Elite • 206

Spetsnaz: Russia's Special Forces

MARK GALEOTTI

ILLUSTRATED BY JOHNNY SHUMATE

Series editor Martin Windrow

OSPREY PUBLISHING
Bloomsbury Publishing Plc

Kemp House, Chawley Park, Cumnor Hill, Oxford OX2 9PH, UK
1385 Broadway, 5th Floor, New York, NY 10018, USA
29 Earlsfort Terrace, Dublin 2, Ireland

OSPREY is a trademark of Osprey Publishing, a division of
Bloomsbury Publishing Plc – Email: info@ospreypublishing.com

A CIP catalog record for this book is available from the British Library

Print ISBN: 978 1 47280 722 9
PDF ebook ISBN: 978 1 4728 0723 6
ePub ebook ISBN: 978 1 4728 0724 3

Editor: Martin Windrow
Maps by JB Illustrations
Index by Alan Rutter
Typeset in Sabon and Myriad Pro
Originated by PDQ Media, Bungay, UK
Printed and bound in India by Replika Press Private Ltd.

22 23 24 25 26   10 9 8 7

Osprey Publishing is supporting the Woodland Trust, the UK's leading
woodland conservation charity, by funding the dedication of trees.

www.ospreypublishing.com
To find out more about our authors and books visit our website. Here you
will find extracts, author interviews, details of forthcoming events and the
option to sign-up for our newsletter.

AUTHOR'S NOTE

Translating out of Cyrillic always poses challenges. I have chosen to
transliterate names as they are pronounced, and I have also ignored the
diacritical "soft" and "hard" signs found in the original. The only exceptions
are names that have acquired common forms in English – for example, I use
the spelling "Gorbachev" rather than the phonetically correct "Gorbachov."

Glossary of acronyms used in this text:

ChON	*Chast osobogo naznacheniya* – Special Purpose Unit
FSB	*Federalnaya sluzhba bezopasnosti* – Federal Security Service
GRU	*Glavnoye razvedyvatelnoye upravleniye* – Main Intelligence Directorate (of the General Staff), military intelligence
KGB	*Komitet gosudarstvenny besopasnosti* – Committee of State Security
KSO	*Komanda spetsialnogo naznacheniya* – Special Operations Command
MVD	*Ministerstvo vnutrennikh del* – Ministry of Internal Affairs
NKVD	*Narodny komissariat vnutrennikh del* – People's Commissariat of Internal Affairs
ObrON	*Otdelnaya brigada osobennogo naznacheniya* – Independent Special Purpose Brigade (of Interior Troops)
oBrSn	*Otdelnaya brigada spetsialnogo naznacheniya* – Independent Special Purpose Brigade (of Spetsnaz)
OGBM	*Otdelny Gvardeisky Batalon Minyerov* – Independent Guards Sapper Battalion
OGPU	*Obyedinyonnoye gosudarstvennoye politicheskoye upravleniye* – Joint State Political Directorate
OKSVA	*Ogranichenny Kontingent Sovietskikh Voisk v Afganistane* – Limited Contingent of Soviet Forces in Afghanistan
omrpSpN	*Otdelny morskoy razvedyvatelny punkt Spetsialnogo naznacheniya* – Independent Special Purpose Naval Reconnaissance Point (Naval Spetsnaz brigade)
ooSn	*Otdelny otryad spetsialnogo naznacheniya* – Independent Special Purpose Detachment (effectively, a Spetsnaz battalion)
opSn	*Otdelny polk spetsialnogo naznacheniya* – Independent Special Purpose Regiment
orSn	*Otdelnaya rota spetsialnogo naznacheniya* – Independent Special Purpose Company (of Spetsnaz)
orrSn	*Otdelnaya razvedyvatelnaya rota spetsialnogo naznacheniya* – Independent Special Purpose Reconnaissance Company
Spetsgruppa	Generic term for a special forces group (plural, *spetsgruppy*)
Spetsnaz	*Spetsialnogo naznacheniya* – of Special Purpose, or Designation – i.e. special forces
TsSN	*Tsentr spetsialnogo naznacheniya* – Special Purpose Center
VDV	*Vozdushno-desantnye voiska* – Air Assault Troops (paratroopers)
VV	*Vnutrenniye voiska* – Internal Troops (under Ministry of Internal Affairs)

CONTENTS

SPETSNAZ: RUSSIA'S SPECIAL FORCES

INTRODUCTION

The *Spetsnaz*, Russia's military special forces, have earned an extraordinary reputation for effectiveness, ferocity, and skill. At the same time they are little understood, and are often mythologized both in Russia and the West. There is an assumption that they are a force of soldiers to rival Britain's SAS or the US Delta Force (some of them are; most are not). There are tales of covert assassinations and macho heroics, feeding a belief that they are simultaneously soldiers, spies, and saboteurs (a few do perform in all three roles, but most are best considered simply as well-trained intervention forces).

The Spetsnaz are, to be sure, an effective force, whose soldiers were the best the former Soviet military could field, and who maintain those standards in today's Russian Federation forces. They have been the "tip of the spear" in Moscow's military interventions and operations for many decades, from early Bolshevik units sent to fight insurgency in Central Asia in the 1920s, through covert deployments in the Spanish Civil War, to running partisans during World War II, and leading the invasions of Czechoslovakia in 1968 and Afghanistan in 1979. Since the collapse of the Soviet Union in 1991 they have fought in Chechnya, in Central Asia and, most recently, in Ukraine. (In another sense, they have also faced "turf wars" launched by other agencies resentful of their control by the GRU military intelligence directorate.) Increasingly, the Spetsnaz are at the heart of a new Russian way of war that emphasizes speed, surprise, and deception over massive conventional force, and their skills ensure that they will maintain their special status into the future.

Indeed, in many ways the Spetsnaz concept is a counterpoint to the traditional strengths and weaknesses of the Russian Army: large, determined, but also lumbering, and lacking in initiative and élan. As Stephen Zaloga notes in his book *Inside the Blue Berets*, the visionary 17th-century Tsar Peter the Great had written of his dream of a "flying corps... a force so constituted that it can act without encumbrance in every direction, and send back reliable information of the enemy's doings... at the disposal of the general, whether to cut off the enemy, deprive him of a pass, attack his rear, or fall on his territory and make a diversion." In the Spetsnaz the Soviets and Russians acquired just such a force.

Their name comes from a contraction of *spetsialnoye naznacheniya*, "of special designation" or "of special purpose." In a sense, this is quite a significant detail. They are not "special forces" as such in the Western sense,

which places the emphasis on the specialness of the operators themselves. Instead, what is distinctive is the special role that is assigned to these troops. After all, for the whole history of the Spetsnaz many or most have been conscripts, and by the rarefied selection standards of Western elite forces most do not really compare. They were and are substantially more dedicated and specialized, and better trained and disciplined, than the bulk of the armed forces – but that has not always been a particularly high bar to surmount. For example, in Chechnya in the 1990s they were essentially used (and wasted) as regular infantry, often for the simple reason that so few regular Army units were in any shape to fight. However, as was demonstrated by their part in the near-bloodless seizure of Crimea in 2014, the Spetsnaz are certainly effective in much more supple roles.

Traditionally, they were primarily concerned with battlefield reconnaissance, shattering enemy chains of command and lines of supply, and targeting NATO tactical nuclear weapons. As such, they filled a gap between regular military reconnaissance forces and the intelligence-gathering assets and units of the intelligence and security agencies[1]. Today, however, the Spetsnaz, which are again expanding in size, have a much wider role as the Kremlin's politico-military instrument of choice. As the prospect of mass wars recedes, Russia looks to a future of small-scale counterinsurgencies and military interventions in the so-called "Near Abroad" of post-Soviet Eurasia. It sees in the Spetsnaz a flexible (and even sometimes deniable) instrument which it can use as easily to fight guerrillas here as to support an insurgency there. In the scrappy, messy security environment of the 21st century, a hundred well-trained Spetsnaz can prove more usable and effective than a whole armored brigade.

The seizure of the Crimea in 2014 was spearheaded by the so-called "little green men" – Russian Naval Infantry and Naval *Spetsnaz* deployed without insignia but, tellingly, with the most modern Russian uniforms and kit. These men marching into the Ukrainian naval base at Perevalne are carrying AK-74 rifles fitted with grenade-launchers, and wear the new "Ratnik" model field dress. (© Anton Holoborodko)

1 See Elite 197, *Russian Security and Paramilitary Forces since 1991*

Finally, it is worth asking how we can know what we think we know? Any studies of deliberately secretive services must grapple with this challenge, and in the case of the Spetsnaz the waters have been muddied not just by Soviet and then Russian *maskirovka* – strategic deception – but also by mythology. A heavy contribution to that mythology has been made by a Soviet defector, Vladimir Rezun, who wrote a series of exposés about the Soviet military under the pseudonym "Viktor Suvorov." Entertaining and racy, they also contain much that has since been demonstrated to be exaggerated or downright wrong, especially when he moves into the worlds of military intelligence and the Spetsnaz. However, since the collapse of the Soviet Union in 1991 there has been a growing body of studies, especially in Russian, which have contributed invaluably to our understanding of them as neither 10ft-tall supermen, nor bumbling imitations of the SAS or Green Berets, but as a distinctive type of special forces all their own.

THE BOLSHEVIK LEGACY

Although the Spetsnaz were formally established only in 1950, there was already a strong tradition of special forces to build upon, from elite elements of the original Bolshevik Red Guard through to behind-the-lines commando forces in World War II. The Spetsnaz certainly regard themselves as the inheritors of the long, proud tradition of the *razvedchik*, the military scout; but they are also a product of the rise of the political police – an integral element of the Soviet regime from its earliest days, and a force with its own substantial military assets.

Soldiers who have joined the Red Guard level their rifles at a police post during the 1917 Bolshevik Revolution. The first Bolshevik "special forces" were drawn from among the most ideologically motivated of such recruits.

Aktivki – "active reconnaissance" operations carried out behind enemy lines, often by covert means – quickly became a staple of the Red Workers'

and Peasants' Army (generally known simply as the Red Army) after its creation in January 1918 following the Bolshevik coup of November 1917. The Red Army found itself facing complex and confusing opposition. The Civil War of 1918–22 was actually a parallel series of separate conflicts – against White counterrevolutionary forces at home; against nationalists seeking independence from the former Tsarist empire; against rival radicals such as the Social Revolutionaries; against neighboring countries; and against anti-Bolshevik intervention forces from Britain, the United States, France, and Japan[2]. The Bolsheviks had a small but highly motivated and often capable core of supporters, and had seized control over the main cities and hubs of industry and communications. On the other hand, they were fighting numerous enemies on widely separate fronts.

Commander Alexander Yegorov and Bolshevik Commissar for War Leon Trotsky review Red Cavalry lancers in Kharkhov, 1919. As well as fighting in the vanguard of conventional assaults, the Red Cavalry also performed fast, wide-ranging drives deep into enemy-held territory, disrupting lines of supply, and terrorizing communities that were accused of supporting the Whites.

The Bolsheviks thus needed to be able to keep their enemies off balance, and to know when and where to concentrate their often-outnumbered forces so as to be able to defeat their enemies piecemeal. One response was to place emphasis on long-range raiding and reconnaissance elements operating in the enemy's rear, especially units of the Red Cavalry. Groups of hard-line political supporters acted as counterintelligence and security details at home, and sabotage and agitation assets in opposition territory. For the latter tasks the Bolsheviks established Special Purpose Units (*Chasti osobogo naznacheniya*, ChON), which by the end of 1921 numbered almost 40,000 men. While most of these precursors of the Interior Troops were used to root out real or supposed "counterrevolutionaries," or to provide ideological stiffening to regular forces, some also operated as saboteurs and assassins. Finally, the Cheka, the Bolshevik political police force, had its own military units. As with the ChON, while most provided rear-area security and policing some were deployed as commandos and scouts. The Bolsheviks also actively recruited and supported thousands of partisans in hostile Poland, drawing on local Communists and other revolutionary

2 See Essential Histories 69, *The Russian Civil War, 1918–22*

Khadzhi-Umar Mamsurov, an Ossetian from the Caucasus who joined the Red Army in 1918, proved one of the more energetic and enthusiastic commanders of "diversionary" troops during the 1930s–40s. In Spain, where he operated under the alias "Ksanti," his courage and determination so impressed the writer Ernest Hemingway that some have even claimed him to be a model for the hero of the novel *For Whom the Bell Tolls*. In World War II he organized partisan groups behind enemy lines, and was made a Hero of the Soviet Union. Mamsurov subsequently rose to the rank of colonel-general, and appointment as deputy head of the GRU.

groups, and in July–September 1920 they briefly installed a puppet Polish government in Minsk. Although these efforts failed either to destabilize the country to the extent that Moscow had hoped, or to prevent the Poles from halting the Red Army at the gates of Warsaw in 1920 and driving it back deep into Ukraine, the Soviets' use of local revolutionaries as part of a wider strategy was a harbinger of things to come[3].

From *basmachi* to Barcelona

The Civil War essentially ended in Bolshevik victory in 1922, and the ChON were disbanded in 1923–24. However, extensive mopping-up operations continued at the margins of the new Soviet Union, where Bolshevik support had been weakest and local nationalists, warlords, and bandits strongest. This was especially true of Central Asia, where the Islamic rebels known as *basmachi* would resist into the early 1930s. Again, Moscow deployed not just regular forces, including air power, but smaller units of Red Cavalry and troops from the political police (by then called the OGPU), often working together with pro-Soviet militias such as the so-called "Red Sticks," who provided intelligence and local knowledge.

In effect, two separate strands of special forces emerged during the interwar era, which were later to recombine. The first were the "diversionary" troops, trained for guerrilla-style insurgency operations. A crucial spur was the Spanish Civil War (1936–39), which saw the Soviets supporting the Republicans against Gen Franco's Nationalists. The political police, now called the NKVD, ran such units, but in cooperation with the GRU, the Main Intelligence Directorate of the General Staff. Key figures included Alexander Orlov, who defected to the West in 1938 when he feared that he was about to fall victim to Stalin's murderous purges; his deputy Leonid Eitingon, who went by the alias "General Kotov"; and chief military advisor "Yan Berzin," whose real name was Petr Kyuzis. Kyuzis was an experienced GRU officer who later assumed the identity "General Grishin," and had operational command of a series of sabotage and assassination elements.

The Spanish Republicans were resistant to such tactics, and the Soviets had to lobby hard for them to be accepted. As the tide of war turned against the Republic, and as the Soviets marginalized or eliminated rival groups within the Republican ranks, this resistance dwindled. The operations of Soviet GRU officers such as the Ossetian-born Khadzhi-Umar Mamsurov, who was embedded within the Republican XIV Special Corps, and the

Marshal of the Soviet Union Mikhail Tukhachevsky was born of petty aristocratic stock, but joined the Red Army in 1918. Trotsky accurately assessed his potential, and entrusted him with crucial commands in Siberia and Ukraine. He proved to be an aggressive and innovative commander, who encouraged the development of deep-raiding cavalry forces and later of paratroopers. His arrest and execution on Stalin's orders in 1937 robbed the USSR of one of its most visionary generals on the eve of World War II.

Latvian Arturs Sprogis, failed to change the outcome of the war but provided valuable experience for the future. Indeed, during the 1939–40 Winter War with Finland, Mamsurov formed and led an ad hoc unit including Finnish-speaking Ingrians, known as the Diversionary Section *(Otdel diversii)*, in attempts to snatch prisoners for interrogation. Most of these operations were unsuccessful, but the GRU's Fifth Directorate, which handled battlefield-level intelligence operations, was still favorably impressed with the notion, and would expand the use of such raids during World War II.

3 See Men-at-Arms 497, *Armies of the Russo-Polish War 1919–21*

The airborne troops

The other strand of special forces development emerged with the formation of paratroop units. Mikhail Tukhachevsky, one of the most daring, aggressive, and forward-thinking of the Red Army's commanders, was an early enthusiast for new ways of warfare. When he became overall commander of the Red Army in 1925, he was able to begin its thoroughgoing reform. He was an early proponent of "deep battle," the notion that a modern, industrial war was won not by a protracted confrontation at the front line, but by finding ways to break through and bypass that line and strike at the enemy's supply lines and command centers. To this end (although, ironically enough, he wrote that guerrillas were contradictory to "real" military operations), he was interested in the potential of tank forces, paratroopers, and special forces to create behind-the-lines disruption.

In 1930 the first field exercise involving a parachute drop war-gamed the insertion of 12-man "diversionary" teams behind enemy lines. This was deemed a success, and an initial company was formed, to be followed in 1932 by a full airborne brigade. Significantly, this was called the 3rd Air Assault Special Purpose Brigade: from the first, these airborne units were envisaged as special forces, to be used to exploit tactical opportunities, seize and destroy targets in the enemy rear, and also conduct assassination and sabotage missions to disrupt enemy operations. Tukhachevsky would fall victim to Stalin's growing paranoia, being arrested and executed as a "fascist agent" in 1937, but the process he had begun continued. By the time the Germans invaded the USSR in 1941 the Air Assault Troops (*Vozdushno-desantnye voiska*, VDV) fielded five operational division-size Air Assault Corps (soon to become ten), each including at least one Special Purpose (*Spetsnaz*) battalion reserved for particularly covert or long-range operations.

"Hail the heroic partisans, who destroy the fascists' rear." This wartime poster emphasizes the sabotage activities that NKVD and GRU advisors encouraged the guerrillas to carry out: cutting telephone wires, blowing bridges, and destroying supply depots. Russian culture was rich in legends of heroic peasants rising against foreign invaders such as Napoleon's *Grande Armée*, but partisans required qualities that were not politically acceptable in the rigidly conformist USSR of the 1930s. The previous assumption that the early stages of any war would be fought on Soviet soil was officially abandoned, and when Stalin broadcast a call for guerrilla resistance on July 3, 1941 such preparations as had been made were long neglected.

THE GREAT PATRIOTIC WAR

The Partisans

The Soviets had long considered the possibility, even the likelihood, of an invasion from the West. Back in 1921 the revolutionary military theorist Mikhail Frunze had written about the potential need to prepare to fight guerrilla actions supported by specialized regular units. However, the initial stages of the German invasion of June 1941 notoriously caught the Kremlin by surprise, and with much of the Red Army shattered in the early weeks of war the need for regular front-line troops was such that the VDV were essentially deployed simply as light infantry. Likewise, many of the earlier preparations for partisan war, including caches of weapons, had been abandoned or neglected.

This state of affairs would soon be rectified. Both the NKVD and GRU ran their own partisan operations, often deploying specially trained commanders, demolition experts, and snipers to provide training and operational support for the resistance groups behind Axis lines; in the case of the NKVD, these were

Members of a partisan group who called themselves the "Winners," which was commanded by Col D.N. Medvedev and supported by OMSBON personnel, posing for the camera after a successful mission. Apart from one civilian guide they all seem to wear the paratroopers' pale khaki jump coverall, and *pilotka* caps; two of these are dark-colored, possibly in NKVD blue. (Courtesy of Central Museum of the Armed Forces, Moscow, via www.stavka.org.uk)

often veterans of the Border Guards. The so-called Partisan Directorate (officially, the Central Staff of the Partisan Movement under the Supreme High Command, CHQPM) both managed its own separate groups, and was also meant to provide overall coordination for the resistance[4].

The specialists were drawn from field operators who had worked in the Spanish Civil War (many of them foreigners), from intelligence officers who had traveled in the West, and also from the pick of the regular military. Such individuals often had extraordinary ranges of skills and experiences. For example, Stanislav Vaupshasov was a military intelligence officer who had worked undercover in Polish-occupied Belorussia in the 1920s. Later he was deployed to Spain as "Comrade Alfred," where, amongst other triumphs, he successfully intercepted the messages of his German counterparts. During the war with Finland in 1939–40 he commanded a deep-penetration unit of ski troops, and then worked undercover again in Finland and Sweden. During the war he was assigned to the NKVD; returning to Belorussia, he spent two years behind Axis lines organizing and commanding the local partisans.

The real precursors of the Spetsnaz, however, were the military's diversionary and reconnaissance forces, most often known as *razvedchiki*, "scouts." They sometimes worked directly with partisan groups, but also operated independently. They were administered by the GRU but were operationally subordinated to the Fronts, the largest field commands. Detachments from the NKVD's Independent Special Purpose Motor Rifle Brigades (OMSBON) also helped train partisans, and provided extra professionalism and firepower for especially important missions.

The unsung heroes were the GRU's Independent Guards Sapper Battalions (OGBM), which were attached to each of the Fronts, with an additional brigade held as a strategic reserve subordinated directly to the high command.

4 See Warrior 171, *Soviet Partisan 1941–44*

Drawn from physically tough volunteers, hunters and sportsmen, and dedicated members of the Communist Party or Young Communist League, these "miners" were trained not only in demolition operations of every kind but also in parachute insertion, cross-country orienteering, and radio communications. Before the July 1943 Smolensk offensive, for example, nine teams with a total strength of 316 sappers were inserted simultaneously behind Axis lines to cut railroads to a depth of some 200 miles. Likewise, when the Soviets launched their Manchurian campaign against the Japanese in August 1945, storm detachments from the 20th Assault Engineer Sapper Brigade infiltrated the Japanese lines to seize vital tunnels, while other units were airlifted behind enemy lines – sometimes simply flown into unprotected airfields – to cut their lines of supply and communication.

Viktor Leonov (right), while serving in the Northern Fleet's 181st Special Reconnaissance Detachment in 1942. He wears a non-regulation cap and a *telogreika* padded winter jacket, and carries an SVT-40 semiautomatic rifle. The following year he took over command of the unit, and went on to earn two separate awards of Hero of the Soviet Union. (Bundesarchiv)

The Naval Infantry

Perhaps the most strikingly rapid and impressive emergence of special forces from the crucible of war was to be found in the Naval Infantry, the Soviet marines. Special units were particularly a creation of the Northern Fleet, whose area of operations included the Baltic and Scandinavian waters. There had been some limited long-range reconnaissance operations in this region in the 1930s, but with the onset of war Northern Fleet commander Adml Arseny Golovka soon realized the need for an independent onshore scouting and raiding capability.

The result was the 4th Special Volunteer Sailor Detachment, a unit of some 70 veterans, athletes, and enthusiastic volunteers operating out of the Polyarni naval base. Initially they confined themselves to small-scale reconnaissance operations, platoon-sized insertions by sea or occasionally over land into Finland or, later, Norway. Increasingly, however, the unit – which became the 4th Reconnaissance Detachment under the Northern Fleet central command, and then the 181st Special Reconnaissance Detachment – also began to carry out sabotage missions and raids to snatch prisoners for interrogation.

By the end of 1943 the 181st was being led by Lt Viktor Leonov, one of the most colorful and ferocious of this new elite. After joining the Navy in 1937 he had trained as a scuba diver, serving for a while on a submarine. At the start of the war he volunteered for the 4th Special Volunteer Sailor Detachment, proving his daring and skills and rising to become an effective commander. In October 1944, for example, he led an operation to neutralize a heavily defended German coastal artillery emplacement at Cape Krestovy, whose 15cm guns commanded the entrance to the strategically vital Petsamo Bay on the Kola Peninsula. Earlier attempts to attack the position by air and

A

EARLY SOVIET SPECIAL FORCES

(1) OGPU cavalry squad leader; Fergana Valley, 1923
The Bolshevik political police played a key role in the struggle against Central Asian *basmachi* rebels in the 1920s, and this cavalryman from the Joint State Political Directorate (OGPU) is patrolling the volatile Fergana Valley. He wears the classic *budenovka* headgear in dark blue, and the Red Army's recently introduced M22 field uniform with the OGPU's black insignia and chest tabs with white piping. Note the red triangle of a corporal-equivalent "commander" below the red star on his sleeve tab. His German 7.63mm M1921 Mauser "Bolo" pistol was something of a trademark of the "Cheka" (as successive incarnations of the political police were still popularly called); his saber is of the 1881 cavalry pattern.

(2) NKVD "diversionary" officer behind Axis lines, 1943
The NKVD had a key role in running and supporting the effective partisan movement behind enemy lines during the "Great Patriotic War." This operator, preparing to spring an ambush, is dressed in largely civilian clothing, but his status is demonstrated by the fact that he carries a brand new 7.62mm PPS-43 submachine gun, as well as a TT Tokarev pistol which uses the same ammunition. The German binoculars are the spoils of war.

(3) Major Ilya Starinov, "Grandfather of the Spetsnaz"; Moscow, 1941
This GRU officer, who is credited with laying the foundations for the modern *Spetsnaz*, was an energetic leader who had

participated in the Russian and Spanish Civil Wars before running partisan operations behind Axis lines in World War II. Here he is shown early in the war, after his appointment as Deputy Chief of Staff of Engineering Troops – but with a special responsibility for blowing up bridges and railroads, rather than building them. Under his M31 *bekesha* sheepskin-lined winter coat he wears Red Army officer's winter service dress of a khaki *gymnastyorka* shirt-tunic and red-piped dark blue breeches with riding boots, with the black collar patches, cap band, and piping of his branch of service. Although he would become one of the most highly decorated soldiers in Soviet history, at this date his highest awards are the Orders of Lenin and the Red Banner.

(4) Stamp commemorating Heinrich Rau
Interwar Soviet special forces operating abroad recruited many foreign-born Communists. One such was Heinrich Rau, a German revolutionary who was trained at the Ryazan Infantry School (which would become the cradle of Soviet airborne troops). In 1937 Rau went to Spain as a political commissar and later a battalion commander in the International Brigades fighting Franco. As much a combat commander as a political activist, he exemplified the qualities the Soviets looked for in their overseas operatives. Here he is commemorated on one of a series of East German (DDR) postage stamps depicting German heroes of the defense of the Spanish Republic.

1

3

2

SHUMATE
2011

sea had failed, so Leonov led a company in a secret landing further along the coast before undertaking a two-day cross-country march to Cape Krestovy. There they captured a battery of 8.8cm dual-purpose guns, and used them both to repel a counterattack and to shell the main gun position, forcing the Germans to destroy the coastal guns for fear of their falling into Soviet hands.

Leonov was made a Hero of the Soviet Union following the Cape Krestovy raid, and after the German surrender he volunteered to be transferred to the Pacific Fleet to join the fight against the Japanese. His 140th Independent Recon Detachment was the first to enter a series of enemy cities as the Soviets pushed the Japanese back through China and Korea. At Wonsan, tasked with securing the airport, Leonov and his political commissar simply marched into the Japanese camp with just eight other men. When taken under guard to the Japanese commander, they intimidated him to the extent that by the end of the day the 3,000-strong garrison had surrendered to Leonov's 150 men.

COLD WARRIORS

Immediately after the war it seemed that the considerable achievements of Soviet deep-reconnaissance and sabotage units were going to be forgotten (a fate that also threatened their US and British counterparts of the OSS direct-action teams and the SAS). With Nazi Germany broken, and the Soviets concentrating on digesting the eastern European states that they had occupied, the immediate need seemed to be for security forces instead. Furthermore, the generals were eager to rebuild their tank-heavy strike armies with technologies and lessons learned from the war and the Germans. The OMSBON were largely dissolved, and the concept of dedicated deep-reconnaissance detachments seemed about to be lost. However, they still had some powerful advocates, not least Ilya Starinov; one of the GRU's most highly respected officers, he is still known as the "Grandfather of the Spetsnaz," and he certainly had the pedigree. He had joined the Bolsheviks during the Civil War; qualifying as a military engineer, under the name "Comrade Rodolfo" he had trained Spanish Republicans, above all in the use of explosives; and during the Great Patriotic War, using the codename "Volk" (Wolf), he had likewise organized partisans and trained them in demolitions and mine warfare.

The GRU went through a fundamental reorganization between 1947 and 1950, and in 1949 began establishing Independent Special Purpose Reconnaissance Companies (orrSn), whose role was to operate up to 125 miles behind enemy lines. These were essentially scouts rather than commandos; their training was not particularly specialized, but nonetheless they represented the kernel of the true Spetsnaz. Meanwhile, as the GRU increasingly found itself providing military advisors in anti-Western wars and insurgencies across the globe, a new generation of officers with a guerrilla past and an intelligence mindset would emerge, whom Starinov would train. Later, Spetsnaz would be deployed covertly as advisors, trainers and, occasionally, combat troops in a variety of theaters, from North Korea to Cuba. They would often be included among GRU delegations, both to contribute their distinctive skills and also to study foreign countries and cities in which they might later be called upon to operate.

From battalions to brigades

Once again, it was the Navy that pushed the pace. From 1950 the Third Department of the GRU's Naval Intelligence Directorate formed the first Naval Spetsnaz brigades, one for each of the four Fleets. In Soviet organization, "brigades" were specialized units outside the usual order of battle, able to be deployed independently; these were not really brigade-strength formations in the Western sense, probably numbering fewer than 1,000 men each. By the end of the decade, however, each would also acquire dedicated underwater sabotage and counter-sabotage units including both frogmen and minisubmarines.

In August 1957 the GRU created five regular Spetsnaz battalions, based on the orrSn companies. Each comprised three companies and a command element, and in wartime they would report to the commands known as Fronts. Much of the impetus for their formation was provided by the increasing deployment of tactical nuclear weapons in Europe by the United States. The intention was that these battalions would penetrate deep behind NATO lines to locate and, ideally, destroy weapons such as the Matador IRBM, which had a maximum range of 1125km (700 miles). To this end the new Spetsnaz had to be trained and equipped not just for parachute insertion but also to be able to fight as scouts. Over time, more than 40 Independent Special Purpose Companies (orSn) would be formed, with a total strength of some 5,500 operators, responsible to the Fifth Directorate of the GRU. During this time their main patron was the deputy head of the GRU, who was none other than ColGen Mamsurov, the veteran of Spanish Civil War commando operations. Each orSn was typically made up of three regular platoons and one special radio-communications platoon. In 1957 the battalions were designated and subordinated as follows:

26th Battalion (Group of Soviet Forces in Germany)
27th Bn (Northern Group of Forces, Poland)
36th Bn (Carpathian Military District)
43rd Bn (Transcaucasus Military District)
61st Bn (Turkestan Military District).

As Soviet concerns grew about the extent to which US tactical nuclear weapons neutralized their own advantage in conventional forces, so too the Spetsnaz prospered. In 1962 the five battalions became six brigades, and their training was becoming increasingly specialized. At first they were largely sent to VDV facilities and received scout training, but in 1968 a dedicated training regiment was founded at Pechora in northern Russia, later to be followed by another at Chirchik in Uzbekistan. The Spetsnaz began to be instructed in a customized curriculum, including both rudimentary training in foreign languages and field interrogation methods (the two being closely linked in the Spetsnaz playbook).

Imperial enforcers

The other main driver behind the rise of the Spetsnaz was a growing awareness of their potential value in responding to flare-ups within the new Soviet empire in eastern and central Europe. When the Hungarians rose against Moscow's rule in 1956, Soviet ambassador Yuri Andropov – later to be head of the KGB, and

Yuri V. Andropov, pictured here after becoming General Secretary of the Soviet Communist Party in 1982, had already played a part in the evolution of the *Spetsnaz* from a military to a politico-military force. As Soviet ambassador to Budapest during the October 1956 Hungarian uprising, Andropov had urged military intervention, and later ensured that *Spetsnaz* arrested members of Prime Minister Imre Nagy's government during the crushing of the revolution in November. When he became head of the KGB in 1967, Andropov would create its own *Spetsnaz* force.

A crowd of protesters surround two Soviet T-55 tanks during the invasion of Czechoslovakia following the "Prague Spring" of 1968; the white-painted crosses distinguish them from otherwise identical Czechoslovakian People's Army tanks. *Spetsnaz* forces had seized the airport and other key locations, and helped to secure access routes into the capital, but the mechanized troops then found actually occupying the city to be a more complex and time-consuming task.

subsequently General Secretary of the Soviet Communist Party – drew on Spetsnaz from an orrSn attached to the Central Group of Forces to arrest the Hungarian government as part of Operational "Whirlwind," the Soviet suppression of the rebellion[5]. He was favorably impressed by their ability to carry out their mission neatly and efficiently (two adjectives not often then applicable to the Soviet military), in keeping with his philosophy of using a scalpel rather than a sledgehammer. Their experience in Hungary also contributed to the new manual of Spetsnaz tactics issued by the GRU in 1965.

Andropov would turn again to the Spetsnaz in summer 1968, when Moscow resolved to crush the liberal "Prague Spring" movement in Czechoslovakia. The 8th Spetsnaz Brigade from the Carpathian Military District was deployed to lead Operation "Danube" alongside specialists from the KGB (now headed by Andropov). On August 20, 1968 two unscheduled An-24 "Coke" airliners in Aeroflot livery landed at Prague's Ruzyně airport carrying plainclothes KGB officers, who were met by Czech security officers working for Moscow. After they had secured the runway two An-12 "Cub" transports landed, from which Spetsnaz troops fanned out to take control of the airport. The bulk of the assault force – the rest of the Spetsnaz contingent, and elements of 103rd Guards Airborne Division – then landed. The Spetsnaz took key locations in Prague before any meaningful defense could be organized: the presidential palace, the main bridges, the radio station, and Letná Hill – a commanding

5 See Elite 148, *The Hungarian Revolution 1956*

B

THE COLD WAR

(1) *Spetsnaz* in Prague, August 1968

The *Spetsnaz* played a key role in securing Prague's Ruzyně airport and other important locations in the vanguard of the invasion to crush the reformist Czechoslovakian government led by Alexander Dubček. This soldier patrolling outside the airport wears the jump helmet, coveralls, and striped *telnyashka* vest of the VDV airborne troops, but a few details identify him as *Spetsnaz*. On his Army-pattern webbing he wears a holstered PB silenced pistol; only issued the previous year, this was still very rare, being restricted to KGB and GRU personnel. Out of sight in the small of his back he would also carry an entrenching tool, which the *Spetsnaz* were taught to wield as a deadly close-combat weapon.

(2) Military advisor, Angola, 1976

The revolutionary struggles in Asia, Africa, and Latin America were exploited by the Soviets as opportunities to undermine the West and extend their own power. Many revolutionary movements received Soviet military assistance, and advisors to help them train with Soviet equipment and to plan operations. This *Spetsnaz* lieutenant has been attached to FAPLA, the Armed Forces of the People's Movement for the Liberation of Angola. Maintaining a low profile, he wears that organization's camouflage uniform (Cuban-made, in a pattern

traceable via the Portuguese to a French original), without rank insignia. Standardization of supply was often a problem for FAPLA; the field cap is made in Vietnam, and is in fact in slightly paler tones than the jacket and trousers.

(3) Sniper in Arctic dress, 1977

In case of war the Soviets planned to move quickly into Scandinavia to secure their northern flank and naval routes. To this end, *Spetsnaz* trained for long-range insertions under Arctic conditions. This sniper, on an exercise near Murmansk, wears a white oversuit over his winter-weight field uniform and fur-trimmed *ushanka* hat. Obscured here, he is also wearing leather winter boots rather than the warmer but more cumbersome felt *valenki*. He uses his crossed ski-poles to steady his 7.62mm SVD Dragunov rifle. In this environment he has used the optional battery warmer, simply removing the battery from the PSO-1 sight and placing it at the end of a wire, which he has tucked inside his clothing to keep it warm.

(4) NRS-2 *Spetsnaz* knife

Western mythology has it that the *Spetsnaz* were equipped with a ballistic knife able to fire its blade at a target. This was untrue, but they were sometimes issued the NRS-2 survival knife; this incorporated a single-shot mechanism to fire a 7.62mm pistol round to an effective range of about 25m (80ft). It also had a wire-cutting attachment on the scabbard.

During the Cold War, US propaganda did much to build the *Spetsnaz* myth. This artist's impression from the glossy annual report *Soviet Military Power*, issued by the Department of Defense in 1984, shows a purported *Spetsnaz* training facility complete with dummy US missile launchers for attack training. (US DoD)

height on which the VDV would then emplace artillery. Within a few hours, even as mechanized forces rolled across the border, Prague's essential points were already in Soviet hands.

The *Spetsnaz* mystique

The Spetsnaz were nonetheless still wholly secret. At the time, their role went unremarked in public and their very existence was denied. Spetsnaz units appeared on no openly available orders of battle (even the military postal system knew them only by lengthy numerical codes); they did not march in parades through Red Square, and the headstones of fallen soldiers claimed that they were paratroopers (when they mentioned their service at all). Perhaps as a result, they began to acquire a special mystique amongst Red Army-watchers in the West even before Vladimir Rezun/"Viktor Suvorov" began writing about them.

The few occasions when the evidence suggested that they had been deployed outside the Soviet bloc created disproportionate interest. Thanks to Cuban defectors to the United States, for example, it came to light that in 1975 Naval Spetsnaz from the Black Sea Fleet's 17th Brigade had been sent to Cuba to train local forces. This was actually a common role for Naval Spetsnaz; the Caspian Flotilla's 137th Brigade was specially configured to train allies in Asia, Africa, and Latin America. All the same, this report created a furore, amid claims that the Cubans were being trained to operate in mainland America. After South African commandos sank a Cuban cargo ship and damaged two Soviet vessels in Namibe Harbour in June 1986, Naval Spetsnaz were deployed to Angola to protect Soviet

Naval Spetsnaz units, 1982 *(Independent Special Purpose Naval Reconnaissance Points)*		
Unit	*Fleet*	*Formed*
17th omrpSpN	Black Sea	1953
561st omrpSpN	Baltic	1954
42nd omrpSpN	Pacific	1955
304th omrpSpN	Northern	1957
137th omrpSpN	Caspian Flotilla	1969

Soviet Spetsnaz units, 1982

Unit	Subordinate to	Formed
2nd Brigade	Leningrad Military District	1962
3rd Brigade	Group of Soviet Forces in Germany	1966
4th Brigade	Baltic Military District	1962
5th Brigade	Belorussian Military District	1962
8th Brigade	Transcarpathian Military District	1962
9th Brigade	Kiev Military District	1962
10th Brigade	Odessa Military District	1962
12th Brigade	Transcaucasus Military District	1962
14th Brigade	Far Eastern Military District	1963
15th Brigade	Turkestan Military District	1963
16th Brigade	Moscow Military District	1963
22nd Brigade	Central Asian Military District	1976
24th Brigade	Transbaikal Military District	1977
67th Brigade	Siberian Military District	1984
26th Independent Bn	Group of Soviet Forces in Germany	1957
27th Independent Bn	Northern Group of Forces (Poland)	1957
36th Independent Bn	Transcarpathian Military District	1957
43rd Independent Bn	Transcaucasus Military District	1957
61st Independent Bn	Turkestan Military District	1957
670th Independent Co	Central Group of Forces (Czechoslovakia)	1981

merchant shipping. This led to a widespread assumption that most Soviet advisors abroad were Spetsnaz; this was certainly not the case, but it was true often enough for the myth to survive.

Likewise, reports later began to circulate that Spetsnaz in plain clothes were driving long-distance TIR freight trucks around Western Europe, especially to spy on US nuclear bases such as the one at Greenham Common in the UK. This was largely another Cold War myth, although it is certainly true that KGB and GRU operatives did try to map out these bases, precisely in case the Spetsnaz might be called upon to raid them some day. After all, the Spetsnaz were originally developed to strike at enemy strategic assets. By the later 1970s, for example, the Northern Fleet's 420th Independent Special Purpose Naval Recon Point (omrpSpN) – as the Fleet brigades were now renamed – had a specific role of not only preparing to destroy NATO coastal acoustic stations, to undermine the SOSUS sound surveillance system built to detect Soviet submarines breaking out into the Atlantic, but also to intercept communications in northern waters.

However, just as often the Spetsnaz were pressed into service for emergency operations at home – not because they were especially trained for such missions, or had any enthusiasm for them, but simply because they were unusual among Soviet troops in being flexible, disciplined, and ready for deployment at a few hours' notice. For example, the Turkestan Military District's 15th Brigade was deployed to prevent looting and maintain public order after the devastating 1966 Tashkent earthquake, and again to quarantine affected areas during a cholera outbreak in Astrakhan in 1970 and one of smallpox in Aralsk the following year.

COMING OF AGE: AFGHANISTAN, 1979–89

In many ways the modern Spetsnaz came of age during the conflict in Afghanistan. They were the spearhead of the initial attack, eliminating the Afghan President Hafizullah Amin when the Kremlin decided that he was terminally unreliable; and during the course of the campaign the special forces (along with Mi-24 "Hind" helicopter gunships) became perhaps the most effective weapon against the *mujahedeen*, one that even these incorrigible rebels feared. The Spetsnaz also demonstrated that they had the flexibility to respond to "the large rupture between theory and practice" in Soviet doctrine – the words are those of Gen Boris Gromov, last commander of the Fortieth Army field force in Afghanistan.

The People's Democratic Party of Afghanistan (PDPA) seized power in the country in 1978, in a violent coup that caught the Soviets as much by surprise as the West. The new regime embarked on a counterproductively ambitious program of social and land reform, which quickly galvanized popular opposition. The regime degenerated into a morass of backstabbing and plotting that saw President Nur Muhammad Taraki deposed and assassinated by his rival, Hafizullah Amin. Despite increased repression Amin's government in Kabul was unable to stem the rising tide of unrest, which had spread from the countryside to the cities and even within the army. Amin kept pressing the Soviets to provide military assistance, but ignored their suggestions that he adopt a more conciliatory line. When rumors (of, it turned out, dubious accuracy) began to circulate that Amin might turn to the USA for assistance instead, Moscow decided that he had to be removed and the situation in Afghanistan stabilized.

The "Moslem Battalion"
Once again, Spetsnaz led the way. In May 1979, Col Vasily Kolesnik was sent to Tashkent to form a special battalion from Spetsnaz with at least a year's service, and of Tajik, Turkman or Uzbek nationality. The idea behind

Spetsnaz from the 56th Independent Assault Landing Bde on patrol in Afghanistan, 1987. They wear loose *Berezka* camouflage coveralls, and are armed with AK-74s; the man at far left has an RPO-A *Shmel* incendiary rocket-launcher slung upright on his back, and note the multiple water bottles. (© E. Kuvakin)

this "Moslem Battalion" was that its soldiers had to be able to pass for Afghans. By June the unit had been assembled, and was being given special training at Chirchik. They still did not know what their mission would be, but it was clear that it would be an important one, since they were told not to worry about the cost of the fuel and ammunition they expended – very unusual, as the Soviet economy was already in chronic decline.

The battalion was 550 strong, with a mechanized company in BMP-1 infantry combat vehicles (not usual Spetsnaz equipment, so they needed to draft in soldiers from the ground forces and train them up); two in lighter BTR-60PBs; and a reinforced support company with ZSU-23-4 self-propelled antiaircraft guns and other heavy weapons. Kolesnik appointed his former deputy Hamid Khabibdzhan Khalbayev as its commander, and in November 1979 they flew secretly into Afghanistan along with LtCol Oleg Shvets, a GRU liaison officer. By December 20 the whole battalion had been brought into Kabul, and were officially told that they would be establishing an additional security perimeter around the Tajbeg, the presidential palace. On December 24, however, they were told that instead of protecting the palace

their role was now to penetrate it, to get two new special forces units known as "Kaskad" and "Zenit" into the building, and then to make sure that no Afghan left it alive.

Kaskad and Zenit were separate teams, each of some 35 operators, established by the KGB under Col Grigori Boyarinov and tasked with killing President Amin. On December 27, as Soviet troops were being airlifted into Afghanistan on the pretext of responding to Amin's requests for support, Operation "Storm-333" was launched. As far as possible, loyalist Afghan troops had been immobilized beforehand, but the presidential guard still had to be neutralized. The rapid-fire 23mm cannon of the ZSU-23-4s were used to rake the palace and prevent the defenders from manning their positions; the mechanized company then rushed the defensive perimeter to get Kaskad and Zenit in to their objective. The battalion obeyed all too effectively its orders to prevent defenders escaping: when Col Boyarinov emerged to call for assistance, he was hit and killed by "friendly fire." Nonetheless, within 20 minutes the palace had been taken and Amin was dead, with the "Moslem Battalion" suffering just five fatal casualties. In early January it was flown back to Chirchik, where it became the 154th Independent Special Purpose Detachment (ooSn) of the 15th Spetsnaz Brigade.

A *Spetsnaz* team after a combat mission near the Afghan village of Tokhram in 1988; note the multiethnic composition of the unit. The central man shows the blue-and-white vest of the airborne troops; the soldier at the right has a primitive laser rangefinder hanging from his neck. (© RIA Novosti)

It would soon return, however, as it became clear that hopes that this would be a quick deployment – simply replacing Amin with the more moderate and pliable Babrak Karmal, and overawing the rebels with a show of force – had been sorely misplaced.

The *Spetsnaz* War

Over time, the Soviet commanders in-country increasingly realized that the Spetsnaz were the assets best suited to taking the war to a determined, effective, and fast-moving enemy, who knew their land intimately and had the support or acquiescence of much of the population. By October 1980 Spetsnaz were already beginning to be transferred in to join the Limited Contingent of Soviet Forces in Afghanistan (OKSVA), and the 154th ooSn was initially deployed to control access to the rebel-held Panjshir Valley. The following year the bulk of the 15th Brigade joined the OKSVA, deploying the 177th, 334th and 668th ooSn, and units drawn from other brigades. At first they were largely wasted by being deployed to protect strategic locations, but by 1983 they were coming into their own as rapid-response strike forces, ambushing *mujahedeen* supply caravans and reacting to the rebels' own ambushes and raids. Indeed, the Soviets came to appreciate the value of reconnaissance forces in general; they made up no more than 5 percent of the ground troops in-country in 1979–80, but by the end of the war this proportion had risen to 20 percent.

At first, their *esprit de corps* bred an arrogance that cost them dearly, especially as the dearth of effective forces in the OKSVA meant that they were often deployed simply as light infantry. For example, the Spetsnaz were

These *Spetsnaz* have just captured a number of *mujahedeen* and are holding them until regular forces come up to collect them. *Spetsnaz* were sometimes employed specifically to take prisoners, who were then interrogated – sometimes under torture – by officers of the KGB or their Afghan counterpart, the KhAD. (© E. Kuvakin)

initially less willing to call in air support; and they generally looked down on the regular ground forces, whom they called *mukhomori* (after a poisonous red toadstool) or "little red riding hoods," because of the red backings to their badges. Over time these prejudices would usually fade, not least because the Spetsnaz would often have to work closely with other forces in the kind of combined-arms operations which were necessary in this punishing guerrilla war.

The primary roles of the special-purpose units were reconnaissance, ambush, and rapid response. In the latter role they typically maintained a ten-day cycle: five days on alert, ready to deploy (normally by helicopter) within 15 minutes, then five days' rest. Their ambushes became increasingly skilful and patient, units often spending as long as a week lying low in the

Spetsnaz in Afghanistan

Unit	Location	Original parent unit
Fortieth Army Command:		
459th orSn	Kabul	15th Brigade
15th Brigade:		
HQ	Jalalabad	15th Bde
154th ooSn	Jalalabad	15th Bde
334th ooSn	Asadabad	5th Bde
177th ooSn	Ghazni	15th & 22nd Bdes
668th ooSn	Kabul (Bagram)	15th Bde
22nd Brigade:		
HQ	Lashkar Gah	22nd Bde
173rd ooSn	Kandahar	12th Bde
411th ooSn	Farah	22nd Bde
186th ooSn	Shah Joy	8th Bde
370th ooSn	Lashkar Gah	16th Bde

hope of catching rebels moving from one base to another, or the crucial supply caravans. When an ambush was sprung the Spetsnaz would lay down as heavy a fire as they could while calling in air strikes, artillery shoots, or both. To this end they found themselves working closely with forward artillery and air controllers, and also with both GRU intelligence officers and the Afghan counterpart to the Soviet KGB, the KhAD (later renamed WAD).

The main surge of Spetsnaz operations was in the years 1984–86, when the in-country command echelon (known as Fortieth Army) technically disposed of two Spetsnaz brigades, the 15th and the 22nd; but these were actually patchwork commands, also incorporating elements from a variety of parent units. In addition, the 459th Independent Special Purpose Company (orSn) was based in Kabul as a security and strategic reserve unit reporting directly to Fortieth Army command. This unit was actually of substantially more than regular company strength; it had four maneuver elements of *razvedchiki*, each of them close to company size. Initially it operated throughout the country as needed, but with the expansion of the other Spetsnaz forces in Afghanistan from 1985 it stayed in Kabul city and its surrounding province. During the war some 800 of its officers and men were decorated for their actions.

A typical ooSn in Afghanistan comprised 583 rankers and sergeants, 32 warrant officers, and 48 officers. When deployed in fully mechanized mode they would typically have 33x BTR-70 or BTR-80 wheeled armored personnel carriers and 13x BMP infantry combat vehicles, as well as four ZSU-23-4 self-propelled antiaircraft gun systems (used for direct fire support), and a BRM-1 specialized reconnaissance vehicle. A company would have a strength of 98 officers and men, and as well as the usual small arms and machine guns it would have six RPG antitank grenade-launchers and three RPO incendiary rocket-launchers. In the field the company typically operated in six 16-man teams, with two company command officers. When the Spetsnaz were inserted by air their

C

AFGHANISTAN

(1) "Moslem Battalion" operator; Operation "Storm-333," Kabul, 1979

Spetsnaz of this unit, chosen for their ability to pass as Afghans, spearheaded the December 27 attack on the presidential palace in Kabul, providing access for the KGB teams who assassinated President Amin. This soldier wears the uniform of an Afghan Army officer, but without rank insignia or arm-of-service tabs, and with an early red-and-yellow DRA cockade on his cap. He is preparing to kill a guard with his silenced PB pistol, and carries his AKSM assault rifle slung ready for the main attack. To accommodate the longer pistol he has cut away the end of his standard Makarov holster.

(2) 411th Detachment operator, Panjshir Valley, 1985

The rebels led by the "Lion of the Panjshir", Ahmad Shah Massoud, were among the most formidable enemies of the regime, and the Soviets and the DRA launched numerous operations in efforts to crush them. This Spetsnaz soldier from the 411th ooSn is taking part in Operation "Panjshir IX" in June 1985, with the objective of recapturing the garrison town of Peshgur. The RPO-A *Shmel* thermobaric rocket-launcher was a new "bunker-buster" favored for taking out fortified positions. He is wearing the KLMK camouflaged oversuit, and carries a slung AKS-74U assault carbine for self-defense; the practice of taping magazines together for rapid reloading became common in Afghanistan.

(3) Sergeant, 173rd Detachment, Kandahar Province, 1987

In the later stages of the war *Spetsnaz* would launch "Stinger hunts" along the Pakistan border to intercept parties bringing in US-supplied surface-to-air missiles. This NCO from 22nd Brigade's 173rd ooSn cautions his team as he surveys a possible ambush site. He wears the "Afganka" field uniform over his *telnyashka*, and a two-part Poyas webbing rig. His AK-74 has a GP-25 grenade-launcher fitted; he also carries an NR-2 survival knife, and an RGD-5 grenade – the latter for use either against the enemy, or to ensure he is not captured alive by the *mujahedeen*. This patrol was inserted, and will be extracted, by helicopter; they can thus dispense with the heavy loads of food, water, and ammo that other patrols had to carry. *Spetsnaz* enjoyed greater autonomy than most Soviet soldiers, and this man has taken advantage of that to use training shoes, far more comfortable than Army-issue boots for scrambling about the Afghan hills.

(4) Afghan Medal for Valor

For the first years the official Soviet line – that there was no war going on in Afghanistan – limited the scope to decorate participants, but that would change later. As well as Soviet medals, *Spetsnaz*, in particular, were also sometimes awarded DRA decorations. The most notable of these was the Medal for Valor, awarded only for conspicuous bravery on the battlefield.

armored vehicles would operate as a separate *bronegruppa* ("armored group") fire-support element. In 1987 the 22nd Brigade had attached to it the 295th Independent Combat Helicopter Regiment, flying a mix of Mi-8 "Hip" assault/transports and Mi-24 "Hind" gunships. This was the first time a Spetsnaz unit received its own dedicated air element.

Hunters and raiders

Some Spetsnaz became especially skilled hunters of *mujahedeen* and their supply caravans, and even began to rival the locals' detailed knowledge of the human and physical geography of their areas of operation. Major Hamid Khalbayev, the Uzbek commander of the "Moslem Battalion" and then the 154th ooSn, became a legendary figure; tales abounded of his "night walks," when he would wander alone among the Afghans armed only with knife and pistol, stalking rebels. These stories (which may well have been thoroughly embroidered) claimed that he racked up 24 kills during such personal sorties.

The appearance on the battlefield of US-made Stinger shoulder-fired surface-to-air missiles, giving the *mujahedeen* a greatly increased capability against low-flying Soviet helicopters and aircraft, had an immediate impact on operations. Although by no means the war-winning weapon claimed by some, the Stinger did force the Soviets to change their methods, fitting countermeasures to their aircraft and flying higher. It also gave the Spetsnaz a new target, and "Stinger hunts" became a favored mission. Captain Sergei Breslavsky of the 334th ooSn, an experienced caravan-hunter, was made Hero of the Soviet Union for being perhaps the first to capture a Stinger.

A key strength of the Spetsnaz was the degree to which their selection, training, and *esprit de corps* allowed them to operate with far greater independence than the rest of the Soviet military (an organization in which initiative was typically discouraged). Sometimes this even led to unsanctioned operations, such as the 1986 Krer raid, a revenge attack against a sizeable and well-defended guerrilla base on the border with Pakistan.

Krer was a constant thorn in the side of the Soviet and Afghan forces as a resupply, coordination and forward base area. After the near-massacre of a

These *Spetsnaz* from 56th Independent Assault Landing Bde, operating in Wardak Province, are interrogating a local following an attack on the unit launched from a nearby village. Note the civilian "trainers" worn by one soldier; and the slung AKS-47, sometimes favored over the AK-74 for the stopping-power of its heavier round. (© E. Kuvakin)

A range of special forces operated in Afghanistan, including elements of the KGB Border Troops. Here Igor Morozov (left), a KGB officer from the Kaskad unit that took part in Operation "Storm-333," sits on a BTR-60 armored personnel carrier in Faizabad, 1982. He wears casual clothing, but carries a slung AK-74. Morozov became one of the unofficial bards of the war. (YouTube/Ofitsersky Romans)

company of the 15th Spetsnaz Brigade in February 1985 the brigade commander, LtCol Boris Babushkin, had nurtured hopes of reprisal, and chafed under his orders to avoid operations within 5km (3 miles) of the border without direct instructions from Fortieth Army. In January 1986, raids by operators from the 334th ooSn not only helped map out the rugged approaches to the enemy base but also took prisoners. One who was induced to provide intelligence – a "tongue," in Soviet parlance – gave up enough additional information about the base's defenses that Babushkin thought a raid was possible. So far he had been operating with the authorization of Fortieth Army to gather intelligence near Krer, but he then used this leeway to plan a full-blown raid in March, after the worst of the winter snows.

Colonel Babushkin's plan called for Spetsnaz from the 334th and 154th ooSn, supported by KhAD security troops, and artillery from the regular Soviet 66th Independent Motor Rifle Brigade in Jalalabad, to scale and seize a ridge overlooking the *mujahedeen* positions, and then to rain fire down on them. In the event, as usual, plan and reality soon diverged: the Spetsnaz were understrength thanks to a hepatitis epidemic; elements of the 334th got lost and were delayed; and the commander at Krer, Assadullah, was able to slip back into Pakistan to raise a relief force from *mujahedeen* there. The Spetsnaz were able to seize Krer, but were then trapped by the counterattack. Eventually Babushkin requested helicopter fire-support and casevac, at the cost of admitting to the higher command what he had done; but when gunships arrived they were constrained by the rules of engagement to making passes without opening fire, in the hope of rattling the rebels.

However, helicopter pilots also tend to be mavericks, and their close interactions with the Spetsnaz counted for something. After refusing to open fire because of orders – and ensuring that those responses had been logged – they then switched off their flight recorders and engaged the rebels with guns and rockets, providing cover for the Spetsnaz to retreat. Meanwhile, the 66th Brigade's specialized air-assault battalion was airlifted into the area to support their withdrawal and the extraction of the wounded. Overall, the mission was a Pyrrhic victory at best: Krer was taken, but ended up back in rebel hands; the Spetsnaz lost some 50 men, and Babushkin was cashiered.

Nonetheless, Krer is remembered with pride among veterans of the 15th Brigade. It proved that the Spetsnaz, unlike the bulk of the Soviet Army, was not dependent on its armored vehicles, and could take the battle to the enemy in their home territory. It also speaks to the Spetsnaz willingness to bend or

Soviet forces withdrawing from Afghanistan in 1989, seen here crossing the so-called "Friendship Bridge" across the Amu Darya river back into the USSR at Termez, Uzbekistan. The *Spetsnaz* were now faced with a dilemma as to how far to incorporate the lessons of Afghanistan, given that the high command did not expect to have to fight such a war again. (© RIA Novosti)

break the rules in the name of striking back at those who challenge them. As one former operator put it: "The generals may sometimes get exasperated with us because we are not pawns on their chessboard, waiting to be moved; but they also know that when there is a fight, there is no one like the Spetsnaz."

Withdrawal

Following the signing of the 1988 Geneva Accords, which committed the Soviets to a phased withdrawal from Afghanistan between May 15, 1988 and February 15, 1989, combat operations were generally scaled down. Most Spetsnaz units left in May and August 1988, although the 177th and 668th ooSn stayed on in Kabul until February 1989. Throughout the nine years and two months of the war the Spetsnaz had suffered more than 750 dead and missing (including officers detached as military advisors), and no fewer than seven became Heroes of the Soviet Union, four of them posthumously:

Col Vasily Kilesnik (1980)
Lt Nikolai Kuznetsov (1985, posthumous)
Pvt Valery Arsyonov (1986, posthumous)
Pvt Yuri Mirolyubov (1988)
SrLt Oleg Onishchuk (1988, posthumous)
JrSgt Yuri Islamov (1988, posthumous)
Capt Yaroslav Goroshko (1988).

However, the Spetsnaz as a whole had also truly come into their own as a versatile, fast-moving, and hard-hitting force that could do more than just deep reconnaissance and sabotage. They had proved their ability to take on counterinsurgency, ambush, rapid-response, and covert operations.

After Afghanistan

In the 1980s, military thinkers such as Chief of the General Staff Gen Nikolai Ogarkov had clearly envisaged a wider role for the Spetsnaz, akin to the missions undertaken by Western special forces. Even so, such were the rivalries between services that even he often had to encode his views between the lines of more conventional writings about the Spetsnaz as equalizers in a future struggle with NATO. For all this, the Soviet withdrawal from Afghanistan was meant to help end the Cold War, as Soviet President Mikhail Gorbachev pushed forward his *perestroika* reform program. Indeed, in 1988, Spetsnaz from the 14th Brigade even took part in joint training exercises with US forces in Alaska.

However, the Soviet Union was lurching deeper into crisis, and Gorbachev's efforts were only accelerating this process. As a result, the Spetsnaz also found themselves undertaking new missions at home – often unwelcome ones. The Spetsnaz were now being pressed into service providing security for government officials, especially on trips abroad, where they supplied an extra dimension to the existing teams of the KGB's Ninth Chief Directorate, the so-called "Bodyguards Directorate." But such tasks did nothing to prepare them for their increasing use as emergency internal security troops.

In April 1989, for example, Spetsnaz from the 173rd ooSn (only just back from Afghanistan) were deployed as part of a force that violently dispersed

January 1990: Soviet Army and Interior Ministry *Spetsnaz* deploy on the streets of Baku, capital of Soviet Azerbaijan, following massive protests and anti-Armenian pogroms. The resulting bloodshed helped push Azerbaijan into seeking independence from the USSR.

protesters in the Georgian capital, Tbilisi, leading to 19 deaths. Meanwhile, others took part in efforts to separate Armenian and Azeri militants who were fighting over the disputed territory of Nagorno-Karabakh. Then, in January 1990, when nationalist protests in Soviet Azerbaijan escalated into violent pogroms against Armenians, Spetsnaz from the 22nd Brigade joined regular police, Army, and Interior Troops units in the "Black January" assault on protesters in the capital, Baku. By late 1990 the Spetsnaz appeared overstretched and disillusioned; this may explain their reluctance to support the hard-liners' coup the following August, which briefly sidelined Gorbachev, but failed to prevent (and indeed, probably hastened) the collapse of the Soviet Union.

SPETSNAZ SINCE THE END OF THE USSR

The dissolution of the Soviet Union at the end of 1991 ushered in a time of turmoil throughout Eurasia. The new Russian military found itself having to cope with an uncertain mission, a massive funding shortfall, and a series of new crises. The Spetsnaz were, as ever, in the forefront, not least in helping Moscow's allies win local civil wars. They had to fulfill this task despite the transfer of units to other post-Soviet states, such as the 10th Brigade to Ukraine and the 15th to Uzbekistan. The 3rd Brigade returned to Russia in 1991 with the last elements of the Group of Soviet Forces in Germany, and was then transferred to the Volga Military District. The 4th Brigade, which had been based in the now-independent Baltic States, was disbanded. Meanwhile, in 1992 the VDV Airborne Forces command created its own special forces unit, the 45th Guards Independent Reconnaissance Regiment, out of the former 901st Independent Air Assault Battalion and the 218th Independent Air Assault Spetsnaz Battalion.

Russia's Spetsnaz struggled to keep their edge in the 1990s. They found themselves being ground between three contradictory pressures: doctrine,

General Alexander Lukyanenko, Minister of Defense of the self-proclaimed Transnistrian Moldovan Republic, takes the salute at a parade in Tiraspol in 2012. Although this small breakaway republic, proclaimed in 1992, has disproportionately large armed forces, the real guarantor of its independence from Moldova has been the Russian Fourteenth Army, later renamed Operational Group of Russian Forces in Moldova. (© Donor)

resources, and necessity. The prospect of a massive confrontation with NATO suddenly seemed to disappear, raising the question of just what the Spetsnaz – originally established to neutralize Western tactical nuclear weapons and command structures – were for. Although Afghanistan had shown their potential, the Russian military hierarchy were anxious to wipe that miserable conflict from their collective memory, and hoped to ensure that the armed forces would never again be deployed in such a war. The innovations pioneered by Fortieth Army – from relying on more flexible brigades rather than larger divisions, all the way to increasing the numbers of snipers in units – were deemed to be *ad hoc* responses to a one-off situation, not lessons for the future. Having lost their old role, the Spetsnaz found themselves being forced to abandon their new one.

Meanwhile, during the chaotic reign of President Boris Yeltsin (1991–99) the military was going through a period of unparalleled financial crisis as budgets shrank, wages were being paid late (when they were paid at all), and forces that were being withdrawn from the corners of the Soviet empire had somehow to be accommodated. The Spetsnaz, relatively expensive man-for-man and accustomed to a degree of special care and attention, seemed a costly luxury in those straitened times.

The GRU appeared to be more interested in trying to salvage its intelligence operations abroad, and the larger VDV corps seemed to offer better career prospects than the Spetsnaz – especially given that Gen Pavel Grachev, Defense Minister in 1992–96, was a former commander of the VDV who promoted many of his old comrades. The result was that able officers sought transfers to the paratroopers, and the Spetsnaz's *esprit de corps* came under serious pressure. Nor were they immune from the demoralization and criminality so rife within the military as a whole. The Moscow-based 16th Brigade, for example, became notorious both for providing "moonlighting" assassins for the organized-crime gangs that were fighting for control of the underworld, and for training hitmen in their own facilities.

This was also a time of crises and conflicts in the former Soviet empire, when bitter if often undeclared local wars challenged Moscow's regional authority. With so many units demoralized and disrupted, the relative handful of elements that were still operational found themselves in disproportionate demand. During the 1992–97 civil war in Tajikistan, Spetsnaz were attached to the Russian 201st Motor Rifle Division, which was deployed in support of government forces against the rebels. Some were also attached to the 15th Brigade, by then technically part of the armed forces of neighboring Uzbekistan but in practice still dependent on Russian personnel.

Spetsnaz also played a minor role in the 1992 Transnistrian War, when the ethnic Russians living along the eastern bank of the Dneistr river seceded from independent Moldova. Fears that they faced forced assimilation into the majority ethnic-Romanian population were deliberately encouraged by Moscow, and this time the Spetsnaz were supporting the rebels. When a ceasefire was arranged, to be guaranteed by Russia's local Fourteenth Army, most of the Spetsnaz quietly returned to Russia, apart from a handful carrying out field reconnaissance missions.

Russian peacekeepers in Bosnia, 1996, as part of the multi-national Implementation Force (IFOR) supporting the Dayton Peace Accords. They have been patrolling in their BTR-80 and are, characteristically, in full combat gear.

Russia sent a brigade-strength unit to join the NATO-led Implementation Force (IFOR) which kept the peace in Bosnia and Herzegovina in 1995–96 after the signing of the Dayton Peace Accords. This 1st Independent Airborne Brigade, based in Ugljevik, was under the operational command of the US-led Multinational Division (North). As a result, it was hailed – and in fairness, should be considered – as an example of the new spirit of cooperation between Moscow and the West. Some of the brigade's *razvedchiki* were rumored to be Spetsnaz, brought into the unit not just to provide much-needed skills but also to use the opportunity to gather intelligence on local and Western forces alike. This is unconfirmed, although elements from the VDV's 45th Independent Reconnaissance Regiment and 22nd Independent Airborne Regiment were attached to the force (and Spetsnaz did subsequently recruit a number of veterans from Russia's IFOR contingent).

All these operations were just sideshows, however, compared with the main theater in which the Spetsnaz would find themselves operating in the post-Soviet era: Chechnya.

CHECHNYA

In the mid-1990s a significant number of the inhabitants of Chechnya – an ethnically distinct and traditionally Muslim republic in the Caucasus, long unhappy under Russian rule – took at face value the new Russian President Yeltsin's offer to the constituent regions of the Russian Federation to "take as much freedom as you can chew." This began a slide toward not one, but two bloody wars. As Afghanistan was to the Soviet Spetsnaz, so the Chechen wars were crucial in the evolution of Russia's military special forces. They acquired a wide range of roles, from hunting rebel leaders to intercepting supply convoys, but they also found themselves fighting an enemy that included many ex-Soviet Spetsnaz among their ranks, leading to some serious reverses[6].

The First Chechen War, 1994–96

On Russia's part the First Chechen War was ill-conceived, under-planned, and badly executed. Following a failed attempt to unseat Chechen President Dzhokar

6 See Essential Histories 78, *Russia's Wars in Chechnya 1994–2009*

Dudayev using rebel and mercenary Chechens, Russian forces invaded the self-proclaimed "Independent Chechen Republic of Ichkeria." Defense Minister Grachev had airily promised President Yeltsin a quick and easy victory, but the forces deployed were too few and in too poor a state of combat readiness to overawe or overpower the fierce and effective Chechen fighters. As the Russian high command desperately sought to retrieve the situation it had to gather genuinely operational forces from wherever it could find them, ranging from the Naval Infantry to the Interior Ministry's OMON riot police. Spetsnaz contingents from across the country were sent to Chechnya, even elements from the Naval Spetsnaz. For example, WO Andrei Dneprovsky from the Pacific Fleet's 42nd Independent Special Purpose Naval Reconnaissance Point was posthumously made a Hero of Russia after his death from a sniper's bullet in March.

Their main role in the first stages of the war was their traditional one of battlefield reconnaissance, but when the Russians stormed the Chechen capital Grozny in 1995, Spetsnaz platoons found themselves being used as shock troops. Their skills were naturally valuable, but urban warfare is notoriously a merciless meat-grinder, especially when the defenders have the skills and time to prepare for the assault. The Chechens' legendary toughness and warlike enthusiasm had meant that they had been disproportionately represented in the ranks of the Spetsnaz and VDV during Soviet times, so they had a good idea of the tactics the Russians would be using. As a result, the Russian Spetsnaz took heavy losses; for example, one whole platoon from Moscow were wiped out when they were lured into a building that had been booby-trapped with explosives.

Faced with shock and anger among the Spetsnaz commanders – and threats by soldiers on the ground, of grave consequences if they were used again in so cavalier a fashion – the invasion commanders began to realize the

D ### SPETSNAZ FOLLOWING THE DISSOLUTION OF THE USSR

(1) *Spetsnaz* operator, Tajikistan, 1992

This soldier serves with the contingent of Russian forces sent into Tajikistan in 1992 to support the government against the United Tajik Opposition, in the early stages of a civil war that would drag on for the next five years. A member of a quick-reaction force being inserted into an ambush site in rebellious Gorno-Badakhshan, he is sitting on a "liberated" Soviet-era UAZ469 jeep, while a Mi-24 "Hind" helicopter passes overhead. He is wearing the KZS two-piece burlap camouflage suit originally introduced for snipers in 1975, and his *"panamka"* hat still bears the now-anachronistic Soviet red star. In the cold highlands he wears a non-standard Asian scarf, which often indicated a veteran of Afghanistan. His main weapon is the 5.45mm RPK-74 light machine gun.

(2) Captain, Moscow, 2006

Identifying *Spetsnaz* often requires some detective work, as no special insignia are usually worn. The decorations displayed on parade uniform by this GRU captain, seen during the 2006 National Day celebrations, suggest that he is no desk officer or intelligence analyst. They are (from left to right) the Medal for Distinguished Military Service, 2nd Class (awarded for 15 years' distinguished service); the Medal for Distinction in Combat; and, most tellingly, the Order for Merit to the Fatherland, a decoration only awarded to officers of lower

than general rank for outstanding performance in battle. On his right sleeve he shows the patch illustrated as 2a.

(2a) GRU insignia

The Military Intelligence service patch, in dark blue with a black bat symbol over a white globe and lettering reading *Voyennaya Razvedka*, "military intelligence".

(2b) Example of unofficial Spetsnaz insignia

In the 1990s, when the *Spetsnaz* were beginning to emerge from the shadows, they largely lacked official insignia, but this shield is typical of the kind of unofficial patch that began to be produced. The blue beret and striped vest evoke the VDV paratroopers, but the half-man/half-wolf image is distinctively *Spetsnaz*, since they take the wolf as their symbol.

(3) *Spetsnaz* "peacekeeper," Transnistria (Moldova), 1992

The terms of the 1992 ceasefire agreement between Moldova and pro-Russian rebels in Transnistria included recognition of a Russian "peacekeeping" force; in practice, this continues to guarantee the borders of the break-away Transnistrian Moldovan Republic. The force was originally constituted on the basis of the Fourteenth Guards Army, but in 1995 it was rechristened the Operational Group of Russian Forces in Moldova, and this OGVM includes a small *Spetsnaz* element attached to its HQ. This lieutenant is wearing the Soviet-era TTsKO uniform in Butan camouflage, under clumsy 6B5 body armor. His SSh-68 helmet is marked "MS," the Russian acronym for "Peacekeeping Forces," as is the patch on his right sleeve. He carries the standard AK-74 assault rifle.

wastefulness of employing them in this role. Most GRU Spetsnaz units (and the VDV's 45th Regiment) had been withdrawn by mid-1995, leaving the 22nd Brigade as the primary force in-country, and 1996 saw it reviving many of the lessons learned in Afghanistan. The Spetsnaz began to be used especially for ambushing rebel forces, launching raids against high-value targets identified by human or technical intelligence, and interdicting supply lines.

The war was proving an expensive embarrassment for Moscow, especially after the Chechens managed to retake Grozny in March 1996. That August the Federal government forces prepared to invest the city again, with threats that they would use strategic bombers and missiles. However, the national security advisor (and Afghan war veteran) Alexander Lebed stepped in, and negotiated a ceasefire with the rebel commander Aslan Maskhadov. The August 1996 Khasav-Yurt Accord and subsequent 1997 Moscow Treaty brought an uneasy end to the war; but it was clear that Chechnya's new status – as neither independent, nor truly part of the Russian Federation – could not be a long-term answer.

The Second Chechen War, 1999–2002

The autonomous Chechnya then degenerated into chaos and criminality, and Islamic extremists began to mount an increasingly aggressive attempt to take over what had previously been an essentially nationalist revolt. In Moscow the government began to prepare for a rematch, not least by making better use of the Spetsnaz. When, in August 1999, extremists of the self-declared International Islamic Brigade invaded the neighboring republic of Dagestan in defiance of Maskhadov's orders, this gave the Kremlin the excuse it needed to launch a new war. The Federation now had a new prime minister, the former KGB officer Vladimir Putin, who was eager to prove himself to a Russian population badly demoralized by the chaos of the Yeltsin years.

First came a massive air campaign, while Prime Minister Putin assembled an army for the invasion. On October 1, 1999 Moscow declared that it no longer recognized Maskhadov's legitimacy, and Russia launched the first stage of a land offensive. This methodically rolled through the northern

Russian Interior Troops (VV) after a devastating ambush on the Zhali-Vedeno road in 2000. The fighting reputation of the Chechens meant that a disproportionate number of the rebels had previously served in the Soviet *Spetsnaz*, and their combat skills and understanding of Russian tactics came as a shock to the Federal troops. (© Svm-1977)

The Chechen Wars saw a renewed interest in snipers among the *Spetsnaz* and regular forces alike. This is the view through the PSO-1 telescopic sight of an SVD Dragunov rifle; the reticle includes markings to allow corrections for range and lead, as well as a stadiametric rangefinder at the left, optimized for a target up to 1000m (1,110 yds) away. The SVD is not particularly accurate, and for Spetsnaz it is being phased out in favor of the SV-98. (© Chabster)

Chechen lowlands before besieging Grozny – which fell in February – and moving up into the highlands. Although the bulk of the fighting was handled by regular Army and Interior Troops, the Spetsnaz played a significant role in raids and battlefield reconnaissance, including spotting for artillery shoots and air strikes. The bulk of the special forces deployed again came from the 22nd Brigade, which as a result was in 2001 designated a Guards unit (the first to be given that honor since the end of World War II).

The Spetsnaz performed their usual roles of deep reconnaissance, interdiction, intelligence-gathering, and rapid response, but with generally greater success and support than during the first war. Not only were more regular forces committed this time, but efforts had been made to improve conditions for the soldiers, their level of training and their preparation. Consequently the Spetsnaz were able to operate as they were meant to do, and scored a number of successes. They were also able to revive several Afghan war practices, such as helicopter-borne "boarding parties" that would watch for road traffic and intercept potential convoys of fighters and weapons. Beyond that, along with the Army's new specialist mountain troops, they were crucial in operations in the southern highlands.

Things did not always go their way, however. In a notorious February 2000 battle for Height 776, for example, a mixed force comprising paratroopers from the 104th Guards Airborne Division supported by a platoon of Spetsnaz from the 411th ooSn was cut off and surrounded by a much larger Chechen rebel force in the Argun Valley. When it looked as if the Russians would be overrun the company commander called down artillery fire on his own position; of the 91 Russian troops, 84 were killed. While a defeat in military terms, the refusal of the VDV and Spetsnaz to surrender when facing overwhelming odds and near-certain death has made the engagement a perverse source of pride, akin to the Krer raid in 1986.

The Vostok ("East") Battalion was an unusual GRU *Spetsnaz* force operating outside the usual chain of command; raised in 2003 from Chechens, many of them former guerrillas, it earned a reputation for both effectiveness and brutality, and was disbanded at the end of the 2008 Georgian War. In 2014, however, veterans of the unit (though few of the original Chechens) were re-engaged by the GRU to form a new Vostok Battalion to support anti-Kiev rebels in eastern Ukraine. Identified by their armbands, these Vostok soldiers attend the Victory Day parade in the rebel capital, Donetsk. They wear a motley mix of uniforms and equipment and carry AK-74 rifles; note the orange-and-black St George ribbon worn around the wrist as a symbol of loyalty to Russia. (© Andrew Butko)

The *Kadyrovtsy*, and the Vostok Battalion

In April 2002 Moscow declared the war to be over, although "antiterrorist operations" continued until April 2009. By around 2005 most military Spetsnaz had been withdrawn from Chechnya itself, even if similarly designated units responsible to the Federal Security Service (FSB) and Ministry of Internal Affairs (MVD) remained. Instead, their missions devolved to local forces that came to be known as *Kadyrovtsy* ("Kadyrovites").

Their rise was one of the key innovations of the Second Chechen War. Moscow's "Chechenization" of the war effort involved recruiting Chechens, including disillusioned former rebels, to form special units able to hunt the rebels on their own terms and in their own territory. These units were sometimes called "Spetsnaz," and often technically reported to the GRU. Most, though, were *Kadyrovtsy* – units personally loyal to Akhmad Kadyrov, the first pro-Moscow President of Chechnya, and, after his assassination in 2004, to his son and successor Ramzan. By 2006 they numbered some 5,000 men in two main units, the 141st "Akhmad Kadyrov" Special Purpose Police Regiment, and the Oil Regiment *(Neftepolk)*, whose official role was protecting pipelines running through Chechnya.

E
CHECHNYA
(1) "Hunter," Grozny, 1995
After the vicious battle for Grozny, *Spetsnaz* were deployed among the forces committed to the mopping-up operation. This officer is one of the handful of *Spetsnaz* dog-handlers who worked with the Interior Ministry forces; his specially bred East European Shepherd – a German Shepherd/Husky cross – is a manhunting tracker. From their vantage point atop a BTR-70 armored personnel carrier they are surveying their surroundings for potential ambushes. The handler has the reinforced brown Gorka Bars mountain suit worn by some Interior Troops, and conceals his identity with a balaclava mask.
(2) Bodyguard, Novye Ataghy, 1998
When the Secretary of the Russian Security Council (and former decorated general) Alexander Lebed undertook direct negotiations with the Chechen leader Aslan Maskhadov, he was accompanied by a team of specially chosen bodyguards. This operator's range of weapons is unusually (and in practice, probably counterproductively) extensive: an AKS-74 assault rifle with GP-25 grenade-launcher, a holstered Makarov PMM pistol, and a slung PP-91 Kedr submachine gun. Over his

Flora-pattern battledress he wears a black Tarzan M24 assault vest. A paratroop badge tattoo on the back of his left hand suggests that he has transferred across from the VDV to the *Spetsnaz*.
(3) Sniper, 2003
Snipers have become increasingly central to Russian counterinsurgency tactics, and this was clearly visible during the Second Chechen War. Waiting in ambush during the mopping-up phase following the official ceasefire in 2002, this *Spetsnaz* operator is wearing a complex camouflaged "ghillie suit" (known in Russian as a *maskirovochny kostyum* or "concealment suit") which he has customized himself. He is armed with the newly issued 7.62mm SV-98, an accurate and hard-hitting bolt-action rifle that is more highly prized than the Kalashnikov-derived SVD.
(3a) *Spetsnaz* sniper badge
The importance of snipers to the *Spetsnaz* operations in Chechnya was recognized by their increasingly sporting an unofficial but tacitly tolerated patch, featuring the GRU's bat above the silhouette of a Dragunov rifle and the crosshairs of a telescopic sight.

СНАЙПЕР

СТРЕЛКОВЫЙ ВЗВОД

While Ramzan Kadyrov brought his forces under the Chechen Interior Ministry (and closer into his personal orbit), there were also, for a time, two autonomous Chechen units formed and funded by the GRU: the Zapad ("West") and Vostok ("East") battalions, formed in 2002 and 2003 respectively. After Vostok had been deployed in South Ossetia during the brief Georgian War, the official disbandment of both these units at the end of 2008 marked the final consolidation of Kadyrov's personal control over Chechnya's security forces. (Vostok made an unexpected reappearance, at least in name, in eastern Ukraine in 2014, though this time the GRU apparently soon dispensed with most or all of the original Chechen personnel.) These units were tough and effective counterinsurgency and security assets, able to operate in the highlands of the North Caucasus as well as any rebels. They were, however, prone to indiscipline and "unorthodox" methods, and were repeatedly accused of abuses by domestic and international human-rights organizations. They were not Spetsnaz in the true sense of the word.

THE MODERN *SPETSNAZ*

Although Spetsnaz would continue to operate in Chechnya sporadically after the end of the main military phase in 2002, they again found themselves in an uncertain position. They had demonstrated their value in the kind of low-intensity, highly mobile brushfire conflicts that look set to dominate the early decades of the 21st century. On the other hand, the regular ground forces and the VDV, jealous alike of their budgets and roles, were disinclined to acknowledge that the Spetsnaz could do what they could not – and what those services did not want to touch, the FSB and MVD wanted to claim for themselves. The 2000 Military Doctrine, the foundational document on which Russia bases its military planning, acknowledged the threats of terrorism, and instability on the country's borders; but the security apparatus claimed that the former was in their jurisdiction, while the VDV claimed to be the best suited for dealing with the latter.

As a result, the Spetsnaz continued to be in the ironic position of being glorified in public (in 2002 there was even a Russian television miniseries called *Spetsnaz*, which showed them as heroic figures doing everything from

Spetsnaz are often employed to test new weapons systems. This operator in a winter snowsuit is aiming an AN-94 rifle fitted with the GP-25 grenade-launcher. In the main they were enthusiastic about this weapon, but a combination of political and economic obstacles limited its procurement. (© Vladimir Makarov)

"To find, and not let go. Together against terrorism!" is the exhortation on this poster, with the bat-on-the-globe insignia of the GRU at bottom right. (© Vitaly Kuzmin)

thwarting terrorist financiers to rescuing hostages), but still marginalized within the military. In their favor, this was a time when President Putin was dramatically scaling up defense expenditure; this helped the Spetsnaz both to recruit more career ("contract") soldiers to reduce the proportion of conscripts in their ranks, and to develop their training programs and facilities. They also often found themselves being selected to test new weapons systems earmarked for wider use, and they played a significant role in the design of the new Ratnik ("Warrior") personal equipment suite introduced in 2013. Surprisingly, however, it would be Russia's war with Georgia in August 2008 – which lasted less than a week – that would consolidate the position of the Spetsnaz, in a new Russian military that was finally freeing itself from its Cold War preoccupations with major land wars in Europe or Asia.

Georgia, 2008

The anti-Georgian rebel regions of South Ossetia and Abkhazia had long been a frustration for the Georgian government in Tbilisi. Eager to teach the outspokenly anti-Russian President Mikheil Saakashvili a lesson that would not be lost on other post-Soviet leaders who might think of challenging Moscow's regional hegemony, the Kremlin encouraged its local allies to provoke the Georgians. After months of cross-border raids, sniping, and even artillery attacks, Tbilisi rose to the bait and invaded South Ossetia on August 7, 2008. The next morning Russian forces from Fifty-Eighth Army began rolling into South Ossetia, claiming that they were there to restore the peace; simultaneously the Black Sea Fleet began blockading the Georgian coast, sinking a Georgian missile boat that challenged the Russian flotilla.

On August 12 the Kremlin declared an end to military operations. The

Spetsnaz scouts led the Russian deployment into Georgia in 2008; their ability to locate and identify opposing forces was highlighted as a success of this days-long clash, even though the ability of the rest of the invasion force to use that information was often limited. These masked operators are wearing the Les woodland-pattern combat dress originally developed for the Interior Troops. (© Alexei Yermolov)

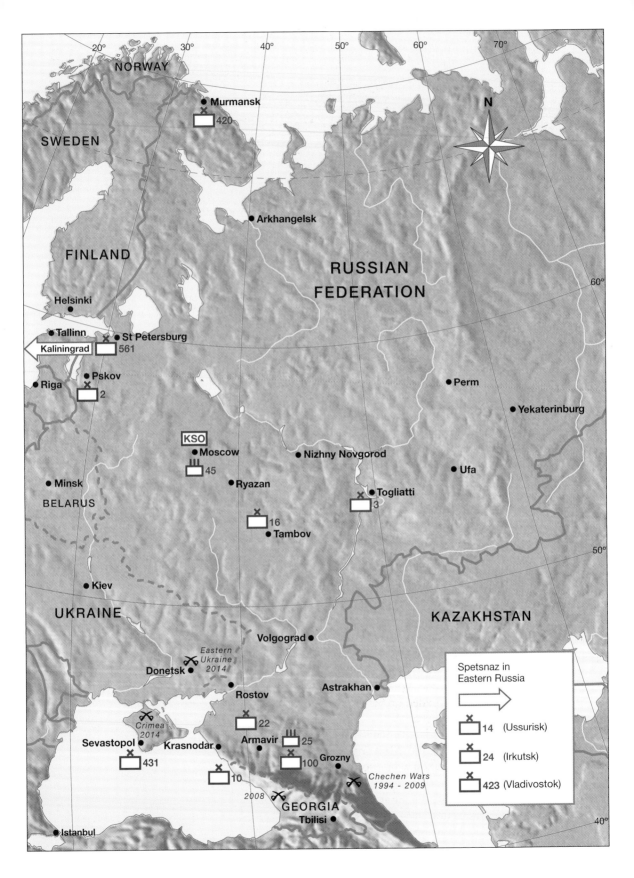

NORWAY

SWEDEN

● Murmansk
✕
□ 420

● Arkhangelsk

FINLAND

RUSSIAN
FEDERATION

● Helsinki

● Tallinn   ● St Petersburg
Kaliningrad □ 561
✕

● Riga   ● Pskov
✕
□ 2

● Perm

● Yekaterinburg

KSO
● Moscow
□ 45

● Nizhny Novgorod

● Ufa

● Minsk
● Ryazan

BELARUS

✕
□ 16
● Tambov

● Togliatti
✕
□ 3

50°

● Kiev

UKRAINE

KAZAKHSTAN

● Volgograd

Eastern
Ukraine
2014
● Donetsk

● Astrakhan

● Rostov
✕
□ 22

Crimea
2014

● Sevastopol   ● Krasnodar
□ 431   ● Armavir   ● Grozny
□ 25
□ 100
✕
□ 10

Chechen Wars
1994 - 2009

2008
GEORGIA
● Tbilisi

● Istanbul

Spetsnaz in
Eastern Russia

□ 14 (Ussurisk)
✕

□ 24 (Irkutsk)
✕

□ 423 (Vladivostok)
✕

40

Russians had driven the Georgians out of Abkhazia and South Ossetia and set up self-proclaimed independent states in both regions. (These are really protectorates: the international community has generally failed to recognize them, but their sovereignty is guaranteed by Russian troops and bases.) The Georgian military had been mauled, and Moscow had proved that its willingness to use its military strength should not be underestimated. Had it wanted to, it could easily have struck at Tbilisi and gone much further into Georgia.

However, while this was a Russian victory, there had never been any question as to which country would win: Fifty-Eighth Army alone had more than twice as many troops and five times as many tanks as the entire Georgian military. Instead, the issue was how easily the Russians would win, and even after eight years of Putin's inflated defense spending the operation actually revealed severe shortcomings. Obsolete, insecure, and often unreliable command, control, and communications systems led to "friendly-fire" incidents, with officers being forced to use their personal cellphones instead. The Air Force failed to achieve the kind of convincing air superiority that was expected, and problems in coordination meant that their aircraft several times came under fire from Russian troops or allied South Ossetian militias who mistook them for Georgian. Although Moscow denies this, credible accounts suggest that three of the six aircraft lost fell to such "friendly fire."

Most of the actual fighting ended up being done by paratroopers from the 76th and 98th Airborne Divisions, with a disproportionate role also being played by the VDV's 45th Guards Independent Reconnaissance Regiment, as well as Spetsnaz from the 10th and 22nd Brigades. Although the GRU as a whole did not come out of the war well (not least, because stale intelligence that they provided led to several unoccupied Georgian airfields being bombed), the Spetsnaz themselves did demonstrate their usual field skills.

As the Russian armed forces slowly modernize and adapt to a future likely to be driven by power-projection, counterinsurgency and antiterrorist operations, the role of the Spetsnaz is increasing, but this has provoked

OPPOSITE
Current distribution of major *Spetsnaz* units in European Russia.

41

Scouts from the 27th Independent Motor Rifle Brigade, in demonstration rather than combat order. Over their Berezka camouflage coveralls they wear only chest-pouch rigs, without the body armor and other kit that would be worn in the field. (© Vitaly Kuzmin)

envious wrangling. After playing a significant part in the success of the 2008 Georgia operation, in 2011 they lost their special status as reporting directly to the Main Intelligence Directorate of the General Staff (GRU), and were formally attached to regional all-arms commands. In part this reflected wider political pressures on the GRU, but also a growing awareness of the importance of the Spetsnaz in future warfare, and a desire to make them the focus of most operations.

Special Operations Command

There had been suggestions for years that the GRU should focus on military espionage, while the Spetsnaz – as tools for battlefield reconnaissance – should instead be subordinated directly to field commands. The experience of the Georgian War only strengthened the case of those who argued for closer integration with the field forces.

To this end, in 2010 it was announced that the Spetsnaz brigades would be transferred to the four Military Districts, which would become Operational Commands in time of war. Meanwhile, the Senezh training and operations center at Solnechnogorsk would be taken away from the GRU and report instead to the General Staff, under first Gen Medoyev, then Gen

Spetsnaz snipers are trained to a far higher standard than those of most of the rest of the Russian military. Like specialists in other armies, they are given considerable latitude in manufacturing and modifying their personal "ghillie suits." (© Vitaly Kuzmin)

Spetsnaz must operate in a wide range of environments. Here a patrol of airborne reconnaissance troops ford a river, their clothes wrapped in waterproof plastic and their weapons ready for use. (© Vitaly Kuzmin)

Miroshnichenko – tellingly, both of them veterans of the rival FSB's Alpha antiterrorist commando force. Senezh, named for a lake northwest of Moscow, would become the base of a new Special Operations Command (KSO, *Komanda spetsialnogo naznacheniya*), including an opSn outside the regular brigade structure, a helicopter attack and transport squadron at Torzhok air base, and a squadron of Il-76 "Candid" heavy-lift transport aircraft. The KSO's roles would range from counterterrorist operations in peacetime to sabotage and assassination in war. The need to insure against any potential threat to the 2014 Winter Olympics in Sochi, close to the turbulent North Caucasus, spurred its formation, and that of the Spetsnaz 346th Brigade and 25th Independent Regiment.

The KSO was officially operational as of early 2013, and, according to Chief of the General Staff Gen Valery Gerasimov, it is primarily intended for missions outside Russia, ranging all the way from participation in UN peacekeeping operations to unilateral interventions. Given that President Putin was simultaneously warning that the imminent withdrawal of Allied troops from Afghanistan threatened an upsurge in chaos on Russia's southern flank, presumably deployments into Central Asia were under consideration.

The GRU embattled, 2010–13

Meanwhile, the failings demonstrated during the Georgian War had given Defense Minister Anatoly Serdyukov the opportunity he needed to force the high command to accept radical military reforms. The aim was to move away from the traditionally dominant Soviet focus on a major land war with NATO or China, and instead to create structures able to fight in a variety of different kinds of operations, with greater flexibility and independence. Divisions were replaced by smaller brigades as the basic building blocks of the Army; the emphasis slowly shifted from the traditional tank-heavy forces toward lighter units and specialist assets such as mountain troops, and a renewed effort was made to increase the proportion of career volunteers in the ranks.

The irony is that this brought new pressure to bear on the GRU, since its political rivals were now questioning its role and value (and Russian bureaucratic politics are especially bloodthirsty). The Ground Forces wanted the Spetsnaz to come under their direct control; the Foreign Intelligence Service

Many special forces officers gravitated into nationalist politics. Colonel Vladimir Kvachkov served in the *Spetsnaz* in 1983–94 before being transferred to the GRU staff. In 2005 he was accused of trying to assassinate a liberal Russian politician, Anatoly Chubais; he was acquitted, but refused to condemn the attack. In 2013 he was sentenced to 13 years in prison for attempting to stage a coup. (© Dmitry Rozhkov)

Despite the rivalry between the two services, exemplified by the Airborne Troops' suggested takeover in 2013, *Spetsnaz* often operate with, or under the cover identity of, regular VDV paratroopers. Here a file of "blue berets" deploy at Zhukovsky airbase, also known as Ramenskoye – Russia's test range for advanced aircraft. The machine-gunners in the lead may be from a different unit, since under magnification they can be seen to wear SS-Leto Partizan battledress, compared with the TTsKO battledress of the riflemen. (© Meoita/ Shutterstock)

(SVR) wanted to humble a rival agency; the VDV paratroopers felt that they could do everything that Spetsnaz could; and voices in the General Staff apparatus were questioning the GRU's special status, which gave it a (resented) direct line to the Kremlin. Thus, on October 24, 2010 – the very day when the Spetsnaz were celebrating the 60th anniversary of their formation – the Ground Forces Deputy Chief of Staff for Reconnaissance, Col Vladimir Mardusin, announced their subordination to territorial commands (see above, under "Special Operations Command").

This seemed to come as a surprise to the GRU; its commander at the time, ColGen Alexander Shlyakhturov, was a relatively weak figure who was on near-permanent medical leave. In addition to being stripped of its special forces, the GRU was being squeezed in other ways. The "Aquarium" – its expansive headquarters in Moscow's Khodynka suburb – had had to shed over a thousand officers, including 80 of its 100 generals. There was even talk that the Main Intelligence Directorate would be downgraded to a regular directorate of the General Staff, depriving it of much autonomy and authority.

From that low point, however, the GRU and the Spetsnaz would quickly rebound. General Shlyakhturov retired at the end of 2011, and his successor, LtGen Igor Sergun, proved a much more active and effective chief. In classic Russian style, the GRU now fought a rear-guard action, nominally transferring the Spetsnaz to the Ground Forces but in practice putting the move off for as long as possible. Perhaps the final stroke of good luck for the GRU was the appointment of ColGen Valery Gerasimov as Chief of the General Staff at the end of 2012. A thinker as well as a commander, Gerasimov was an outspoken advocate of a new form of "hybrid" or "non-linear" war, by which Russia could assert her interests through an imaginative mix of political, economic, intelligence, and military operations. The Spetsnaz appeared to be ideal instruments for such operations – but this required them to be strategic assets, rather than just battlefield scouts subordinated to territorial commands.

"Macho" staged theatricals in 2014 on the 20th anniversary of the creation of the VDV's own *Spetsnaz* unit, whose full title is the 45th Guards Independent Order of Kutusov, Order of Alexander Nevsky Special Purpose Regiment. (© Vitaly Kuzmin)

As a result, in 2013 the resubordination of the Spetsnaz was quietly dropped, and they returned to (if they had ever really left) the control of the GRU. This also saved them from a takeover bid by the paratroopers that year, when VDV commander ColGen Vladimir Shamanov mooted that the Spetsnaz ought to be made part of new Rapid Reaction Forces, which inevitably would be controlled by his larger service. This came to nothing, however; and in 2014 the GRU's prestige would rise again with the annexation of Crimea, followed by a semi-covert campaign of insurrection and destabilization in eastern Ukraine (see below).

Organization, 2014

As of late 2014, Russia's Spetsnaz comprise seven regular brigades of various sizes, in total comprising perhaps 19 battalion-size ooSns. They are responsible to the GRU's Fifth Directorate (Operational Reconnaissance), although in the field they are subordinated to operational commanders. The four Independent Special Purpose Naval Reconnaissance Points (omrpSpN, analogous to brigades) are still technically part of the Fifth Directorate, but are more closely tied to their parent Fleets. Beyond that, there is the VDV's own 45th Guards Independent Special Purpose Regiment (opSn), and three other separate Spetsnaz elements. One, the 100th Independent Brigade, is often used as a test bed for new ideas and equipment. As mentioned above, two others were created in 2011–12 as part of the security preparations for the Sochi Winter Olympics in southwestern Russia: the 25th Independent Regiment (opSn), optimized for operations in the turbulent North Caucasus, and the 346th Brigade, which appears to be closer to detachment (regiment) size, and to have become the KSO's operational element.

Recruitment and training

There is constant pressure to try to ensure that Spetsnaz units are made up exclusively of professional volunteers, "contract servicemen" in Russian parlance. This is proving a challenge, however, and while some elements are all-volunteer, as of 2013 some others were as much as 50 percent composed of draftees – albeit the pick of the crop, chosen for their physical prowess and

The very emphasis that the Russians have placed on the use of *Spetsnaz* as deep-penetration elements has led them to devise countermeasures against such tactics. This specialized Taifun-M "anti-sabotage vehicle," based on the BTR-82, mounts an extensive sensor array including radar, thermal-imaging night vision, and echo-location, as well as ECM jammers to disable remotely-detonated bombs and a small surveillance drone, in addition to the turret-mounted 7.62mm machine gun. (© Vitaly Kuzmin)

prior interest in such activities as shooting, orienteering, and sports. Nonetheless, it does mean that most units suffer biannual "churn," with new conscripts on one-year terms entering in May and November (after four months' basic training), sergeants and specialists in July and January (after six months), and junior officers fresh from military colleges every September.

Training is an intense mix of physical conditioning, mental orientation – great emphasis is placed on trying to surprise the recruits, and develop their ability to respond quickly to the unexpected – and imparting necessary tactical and technical skills. Professionals may well learn the basics of a language relevant to their specific brigade's area of operations, but this is not a core issue; there is no expectation that they will acquire anything like fluency, unless they are likely to transfer into the GRU's intelligence operations.

While they receive generally better treatment than regular troops, and will often be in receipt of combat bonuses, the Spetsnaz suffer the usual Russian handicaps of patchy administration and sometimes late pay. Even during the

A Kamov Ka-52 "Alligator" day/night attack helicopter at Torzhok airbase, home of the 344th Army Aviation Combat Training Center, where this squadron has been assigned to provide close air support for Special Operations Command (KSO). It mounts a 2A42 30mm autocannon, and has hardpoints for rocket pods or Vikhr laser-guided missiles. (© Alex Beltyukov)

August 2 is "VDV Day," and since they lack their own special day the *Spetsnaz* also join these festivities. Here, at a parade in Red Square in 2014, veterans from the 5th Independent Special Purpose Brigade wave their unit flag, incorporating the GRU's bat as well as the VDV's parachute. (© Author's photo)

Second Chechen War there were protests about combat pay not being disbursed and promised equipment not materializing. There are also specific issues for ambitious officers, as the highest rank found within the Spetsnaz is colonel, for a *kombrig* (brigade commander). Those with higher aspirations must either move into the mainline GRU structure, which is dominated by intelligence officers rather than commandos, or else make the difficult sideways shift into the VDV, which means bridging a long-standing inter-arm rivalry. In this respect they are much less well placed than VDV officers, who have higher command positions available within their own arm of service, and who can also transfer more easily into regular military command positions or

Russian Spetsnaz units, 2014

2nd Brigade (Promezhitsa, Pskov):
  177th ooSn (Taibol)
  186th ooSn
  unidentified ooSn
  1071st Training Regt (Pechora)
3rd Guards Bde (Togliatti):
  2x unidentified ooSn
10th Bde (Molkino):
  3x unidentified ooSn
14th Bde (Ussurisk):
  282nd ooSn
  294th ooSn (Khabarovsk)
  308th ooSn
  314th ooSn
16th Bde (Chuchkogo/Tambov, Moscow):
  370th ooSn
  2x unidentified ooSn
22nd Guards Bde (Stepnoi):
  173rd ooSn
  411th ooSn

24th Bde (Irkutsk):
  unidentified ooSn (Novosibirsk)
  unidentified ooSn (Berdsk)
Other:
100th Bde (Mozdok)
25th Independent Regt (Stavropol)
Special Operations Command (KSO):
346th Bde (Prokhladny)
Navy
42nd Indep SP Naval Recon Point (Vladivostok, Pacific Fleet)
420th ISP Naval RP (Severomorsk, Northern Fleet)
431st ISP Naval RP (Sevastopol, Black Sea Fleet)
561st ISP Naval RP (Kaliningrad, Baltic Fleet)
VDV Command
45th Guards Independent Spetsnaz Regt (Kubinka, Moscow)

Television coverage of the 2014 invasion of Crimea unveiled to the world the new "look" Russian soldier. These Naval *Spetsnaz* are wearing the Ratnik pattern uniform, including body armor, load-carrying vests, and web gear. A new tactical radio gives them the kind of soldier-to-soldier communications that they hitherto lacked. (© Photo.ua/Shutterstock)

staff posts at the Ministry of Defense or General Staff. This is a long-standing problem: Valery Vostrotin, a highly-decorated paratroop officer who retired as a colonel-general and became chairman of the VDV veterans' association, recounted that as an officer cadet in the late 1970s he turned down the chance to join the 9th Company at the Ryazan VDV Training Academy, which was for Spetsnaz, precisely because it was a career dead end.

Crimea and Ukraine, 2014

The Spetsnaz played a very significant role in the virtually bloodless annexation of the Crimea in March 2014, and in the much bloodier and, at the time of writing, still ongoing Russian-backed insurgency in Ukraine's eastern Donbas region. In the process, they exemplified the new doctrine that ColGen Gerasimov championed, which envisions military force being used with precision, in the context of wider strategies that rely at least as much on subversion, misdirection, economic and political leverage, and intelligence missions.

Political protests at the corruption and increasingly pro-Moscow orientation of Ukrainian President Viktor Yanukovych led to bloody clashes in Kiev, and prompted him to flee the country on February 21, 2014. A new provisional government took power; Moscow, angered and alarmed at the departure of its ally, and fearful that Ukraine would leave its sphere of

---

F   **MODERN *SPETSNAZ* (1)**

(1) Spotter, Georgia, 2008
The Russian operation in Georgia was marred by "friendly fire" incidents despite the deployment of several *Spetsnaz* spotters, such as this officer using a 1D26 "Atoll" laser rangefinder/target designator. The problems were often caused by intelligence not being communicated effectively from the spotters to the artillery and air controllers. This soldier, apparently having trouble with his Akvedukt HF R-168-1KE radio, may eventually have to fall back on using his insecure personal cellphone instead. He is wearing the relatively rare Flectar-D camouflage uniform, and has a slung Vityaz-SN submachine gun as a self-defense weapon.

(2) Sergeant, Mulino, 2012
The *Spetsnaz* have been key figures in the testing of the new Ratnik combat uniform and equipment ensemble. This sergeant, pictured during a combined-arms exercise at the Mulino training ground east of Moscow, is advancing under covering fire from the latest Ka-52 "Alligator" attack helicopter (NATO reporting name: "Hokum-B"), under the coordination of the new (and still unproven) YeSU battlefield command and control system. He is armed with the Kalashnikov-derived AK-12 assault rifle, one of the contenders to replace the AK-74, and his helmet has laser sensors to register "hits" during the war game.

(3) *Spetsnaz*, Moscow, 2014
The annual Victory Day parade through Moscow on May 9 commemorating the end of World War II is always an expression of military might and confidence. Following the seizure and annexation of Crimea in 2014 a contingent of *Spetsnaz* were given an unprecedentedly visible role in the parade. This soldier wears elements of the new Ratnik combat uniform seen in Crimea, with digital Flora-pattern battledress and 6B43 body armor, and goggles on his 6B27 helmet. He carries the VSS Vintorez silenced sniper rifle.

The Soviet Pacific Fleet's 55th Red Banner Naval Infantry Division included a regiment-size Naval *Spetsnaz* force, which became the basis for the modern Russian 263rd Naval Infantry Recon Battalion. Here Pacific Fleet infantry demonstrate their skills for visiting US Navy officers at Vladivostok in 1990. They wear woodland-pattern TTsKO uniforms and their traditional black berets, and carry AK-74s with fixed bayonets.

interest, quickly began making its own preparations. The next day the VDV's 45th opSn was put on alert, as was the 3rd Spetsnaz Brigade, and two ooSn of the 16th Brigade left their base at Tambov.

A key question was the future of Crimea. This peninsula has a majority of Russian-speakers, and had only been (controversially) handed over to Ukraine by Russia in 1954. It was also the base of the Russian Black Sea Fleet, following an agreement with Kiev. Local pro-Russian forces began to form "self-defense militias," clearly backed or even instigated by Moscow working through the marines of the 810th Independent Naval Infantry Brigade already based there. Unidentified men with military weapons began blockading Ukrainian bases, and on February 27 around 50 men seized the Crimean parliament building. While claiming to be a local militia, this well-armed and highly professional unit turned out to be the first deployment of operators from the KSO, supported by elements of the VDV's 45th opSn. The next day Mi-8 "Hip" transport helicopters, escorted by the latest Mi-35M "Hind-E" gunships, flew in Naval Spetsnaz from the 431st omrpSpN.

Landing ships then brought elements of the 10th and 25th Spetsnaz Brigades into Sevastopol harbor, and all Ukrainian bases progressively came under blockade. Over the next week, forces from the 3rd and 16th Brigades and the 25th opSn were also moved into Crimea. This gave the Russians a force of several thousand highly skilled operators, but very little heavy equipment. Had the Ukrainians been willing and able to fight (as it turned out, the provisional government in Kiev was uncertain how far it could trust its own military, and so never gave such orders), this could have been a problem for the Russian invaders, so the priority shifted to deploying more conventional units with armor and artillery elements. The 727th Independent Naval Infantry Battalion, 291st Artillery Brigade, and 18th Independent Motor Rifle Brigade were introduced to provide that heavier support. On

March 16 a hurried referendum in Crimea registered an overwhelming vote in favor of reuniting with Russia, and the peninsula was duly annexed. The Spetsnaz then led the way in the often forceful but non-lethal moves on to remaining Ukrainian bases that led to the surrender or withdrawal of all remaining government troops. One of the last holdouts, the elite 1st Marine Regiment, was stormed by Spetsnaz on March 24; they used only stun grenades and smoke, but were backed up by BTR-82A armored personnel carriers armed with 30mm autocannon, as well as two helicopter gunships.

The conflict in eastern Ukraine – predominantly the industrial Donbas region, with its large proportion of Russian-speakers, and important industrial base – has been a much less surgical venture. There the conflict has been fought largely by local militias, including defectors from the Ukrainian Army and police supported by large numbers of Russian and Cossack volunteers. Many of these appear to have been assembled, armed, and even paid by the GRU, in an operation run from the nearby city of Rostov. Persistent but unconfirmed reports suggested that Spetsnaz from a variety of units, including the VDV's 45th opSn, were deployed at times to prevent government forces from winning a convincing victory against the rebel militias. Central control on both sides may be problematic, since Kiev's forces also include irregular units raised by individual oligarchs. At the time of writing an official ceasefire is being observed only inconsistently, and Russia has been accused by the USA of inserting more troops and armor into disputed areas.

The "other *Spetsnaz*"

It is also worth noting that Russia's Spetsnaz must also cope with the rise of sometimes partner, sometimes rival Spetsnaz in other post-Soviet republics

Although they are rarely willing to admit it, the special forces of most of the post-Soviet states are still heavily influenced by *Spetsnaz* practices and doctrines even if they have sought training and equipment from elsewhere. These soldiers of Azerbaijan's "maroon berets" have received training from the Turkish military, and carry Israeli TAR-21 rifles. (© WalkerBaku)

General Vladislav Achalov, who commanded the VDV in 1989–90, was implicated in the hard-liners' attempted coup against the reformist regime of Mikhail Gorbachev in 1991, and until his death in 2011 he remained close to conservative and nationalist circles. As a "soldier's soldier," Achalov also continued to be a popular figure in the special forces community, and was president of the Russian Airborne and *Spetsnaz* Veterans' Association. (VDV Press Service)

following the dismemberment of the Soviet forces in 1992. Inevitably, at the time this caused all kinds of dislocations, especially as many ethnic Russian Spetsnaz opted to transfer into units remaining under Moscow's control. It has to be said that few of these "new" Spetsnaz have managed to maintain the professionalism and operational capabilities they inherited from Soviet times.

The 10th Brigade, based in Izyaslav, transferred to Ukrainian service, where it became the basis for the special forces that in 2014 have taken part in Kiev's operation against Moscow-backed rebels in the east of the country. The 5th Brigade, based in Mariyna Gorka, came under the control of Belarus; this was a particular blow, since it had been one of the largest units, and its extensive modern facilities included the training grounds where the Spetsnaz had been testing new gliders and microlights. The 15th Brigade was transferred to Uzbekistan, along with the 459th orSn, and the training facility built to prepare forces for operations in Afghanistan, but Russian forces continue to have close links with this brigade and consider it an allied

---

G

MODERN *SPETSNAZ* (2)

(1) Embassy security officer, Damascus, 2013

Spetsnaz may be assigned as security officers to embassies in high-risk foreign cities, or else may use such postings as cover for intelligence and reconnaissance work. This officer, seen guarding the Russian embassy in Damascus in 2013 after the start of the Syrian civil war, wears practical civilian clothing (including a Spartak Moscow football team shirt) under a FORT Hussar tactical armor vest. He carries a rare OTs-14-4 bullpup assault rifle, with a backup Glock 17 in a drop holster. It is uncertain whether he is GRU *Spetsnaz*, or from the highly clandestine Zaslon *Spetsnaz* unit of the Foreign Intelligence Service (SVR).

(2) Airborne recon scout, 45th opSn, 2012

The 45th Guards Independent Special Purpose Regiment is subordinated directly to the VDV Airborne Troops high command, and is employed for special missions such as reconnaissance and the elimination of high-value targets. Formed in 1994, it has seen action in Chechnya, Georgia, Kyrgyzstan, and Ukraine. This soldier, on an exercise near the unit's Kubinka base in the Moscow region, wears a sniper's two-piece camouflage uniform in Berezka pattern; he has

Sbruya-Partizan web equipment, and an SSO Bobr backpack. His weapon is an AKMN, a modernized AK-47 with night-sight bracket, here fitted with a PBS sound suppressor.

(2a) 45th opSn shoulder patch

Since the unit was only created in 1994 the badge reflects a new style introduced across the VDV. The traditional *Spetsnaz* wolf symbol and the unit number are set against the usual wings and parachute of airborne troops.

(3) Close-combat training, 2014

Even more so than most special forces, the *Spetsnaz* place a premium on physical fitness and hand-to-hand combat skills. The latter involve their own variant of Sambo, a distinctive Russian martial art, using not just hands and feet but also a range of weapons including knives and, as here, the versatile and lethal *saperka* short-handled entrenching tool with sharpened edges. He is wearing the VDV's digital Flora-pattern battledress, standard issue since 2011 but soon to be replaced with the new Ratnik pattern (see Plates F2 & F3). The length of ribbon in the traditional orange and black stripes of the pre-Revolution Order of St George is a patriotic symbol increasingly seen displayed in various ways, especially since the annexation of Crimea.

1

3

2

2a

ВОЗДУШНО-ДЕСАНТНЫЕ ВОЙСКА

СПЕЦИАЛЬНОГО НАЗНАЧЕНИЯ

45

ПОЛК

SHUMATE
2014

force. Furthermore, even republics that were not able to lay claim to Soviet Spetsnaz units created special forces very much in their image, such as Azerbaijan's "maroon berets" and Armenia's "black berets."

The future

Having suffered from a degree of neglect in the 1990s and early 2000s, the Spetsnaz are back at the heart of modern Russia's new way of war. Any suggestions that the GRU should be downgraded or the Spetsnaz subordinated to the Ground Forces or the VDV appear to have been buried for the foreseeable future. The perhaps 15,000–17,000 officers and men within various Spetsnaz formations are by no means all (or even mainly) up to the standard of true Western special forces, not least because many remain conscripts. Most should instead be considered as top-quality light infantry, akin to the US Army Rangers or the French Foreign Legion's 2nd Parachute Regiment. Perhaps only the KSO and special elements within the other units, no more than a thousand men in total, would be considered "Tier 1" in Western parlance – in other words, approaching the standard of Britain's SAS or the US Delta and DEVGRU. Nonetheless, that is a formidable asset, and it gives a vital additional capability to a Russian military that is, even after the reforms pursued since the 1990s, a relatively unsubtle force.

Of course, the term "Spetsnaz" also has much wider use in Russia, and it is clear that other police, intelligence, and security agencies will retain their own special (and sometimes not-so-special) forces. Most of these have specialized roles wholly different from those of the GRU Spetsnaz. For example, as described in the present author's Elite 197 *Russian Security and Paramilitary Forces since 1991*, the FSB's Alpha units are essentially

The Alpha *Spetsnaz* units of the Federal Security Service (FSB) are primarily tasked with counterterrorist operations. This team are armed with SR-3 Vikhr subsonic assault carbines with sound suppressors. A subdued-pattern sleeve badge is just visible. (© Spetsnaz Alfa)

Among the *Spetsnaz* elements created by a range of security forces in Russia for differing specialist roles, those of the MVD Interior Troops' Peresvet 33rd Special Purpose Detachment are probably the closest to the GRU's *Spetsnaz*, although more likely to be deployed for counterinsurgency tasks. This operator also has the SR-3 Vikhr silenced compact assault carbine. (© Vitaly Kuzmin)

counterterrorist teams, while the SVR's Zaslon team is maintained for covert operations overseas. However, there are also forces that overlap much more closely with the military Spetsnaz. Not the least of these are the MVD's Interior Troops Spetsnaz, such as the Moscow-based 33rd Special Purpose Detachment, also known as Peresvet; this fought in Chechnya, and is trained and equipped much like its GRU counterparts. Given the Kremlin's traditional propensity to allow, even encourage the proliferation of overlapping forces in order to avoid overdependence on a single agency (a habit born of a historic fear of coups), this is likely to remain the case.

The future for the Spetsnaz is therefore a rosy one, a prospect that does not necessarily please many of Russia's neighbors. Although the likelihood that Russia will achieve its goal of fielding an all-professional army by 2020 still appears remote, the odds are that the Spetsnaz will certainly all be contract volunteers well before that date. As reform actually creates "two armies" in Russia – a small, well-equipped, and versatile operational intervention force of fewer than 60,000 men, and a larger, still relatively unreformed rump of some 100,000 Ground Forces for territorial defense and second-wave security – the Spetsnaz, along with the VDV, will continue to represent the "tip of the spear."

WEAPONS & EQUIPMENT

Unlike many of the smaller special armed elements created by the security agencies, and in contradiction of some lurid tales about their unique equipment, the Spetsnaz do not usually employ imported or specialist weapons (with some mission-specific exceptions). Rather, as units of the regular military, they use essentially the same weapons as the rest of the Army – although they typically get first pick of new types, and also enjoy much greater freedom to customize and "mix and match."

Small arms

The standard Spetsnaz weapon is the same 5.45mm AK-74 assault rifle family as for regular troops, typically AK-74Ms, AK-74Ns with fittings for night-vision 'scopes, and short-barreled AKS-74U assault carbines. This is a generally well-regarded weapon, with much the same ruggedness as the original AK-47 while being lighter and more accurate. In some cases, Spetsnaz prefer the heavier 7.62mm round and so carry the older AKM or AKMN; alternatively they carry the newer AK-103 rifle, which fires the same ammunition but incorporates many of the improvements of the AK-74. The government has repeatedly declared that the AK-74 would be replaced by a new assault rifle, originally the AN-94 and then potentially the AK-12, both of which offer greater long-range accuracy and other advantages. However, although a few of these have been field-tested by the

SPECIALIST FORCES

(1) Naval *Spetsnaz* frogman
Each of the four Russian fleets has its own Naval *Spetsnaz* forces, including specialist combat swimmers employed for covert operations behind enemy lines, sabotage missions, and underwater guard duties. This frogman from the Pacific Fleet is using the IDA-71 rebreather apparatus, standard issue for over 30 years. The Soviets were at the forefront of research into underwater weapons, and the SPP-1M pistol he is aiming is a four-barrel weapon firing steel darts. Spetsnaz frogmen may also be issued the APS underwater rifle, or the newer ASM-DT, a hybrid weapon able to fire either darts or conventional rounds.

(1a) *Spetsnaz* frogman patch
The underwater combat units of the Naval *Spetsnaz* often sport unit- and fleet-specific patches, but this is the standard insignia for the whole arm. It symbolically combines a parachute, a torpedo, and a shark, with the slogan "Duty – Honor – Courage."

(2) Naval *Spetsnaz*, 431st omrpSpN; Crimea, February–March 2014
The so-called "little green men" who so quickly seized key locations in Crimea prior to its formal annexation into the

Russian Federation were largely Naval Infantry from the Black Sea Fleet, including *Spetsnaz* from the 431st Independent Special Purpose Naval Reconnaissance Point. This member of the detail that seized Belbek military airfield displays no insignia – in order to sow uncertainty as to whether they were local "militia" or Russian troops – but there is little doubt as to his identity. He is dressed in the latest Russian Naval Infantry battledress, part of the new Ratnik equipment suite currently being phased into service. This includes 6B43 body armor with a 6Sh117 tactical load-carrying vest, and a cover over his new-model ShBM helmet, as well as one of the new 168-0,5UME tactical radios. While his 7.62mm PKM general-purpose machine gun is a rather more elderly design it is still an effective weapon. On the right side of his chest he also carries a 6Kh5 AK-74 bayonet-knife.

(3) FSB *Spetsnaz* operator, 2012
Among the various security forces also considered *Spetsnaz* in the wider sense of the term, the most elite are the Alpha counterterrorist commandos of the Federal Security Service. This operator has rappelled down the outside of a building and is awaiting orders to commence an assault. He wears an LShZ-2DT helmet and Defender-2 armored vest over black fireproof fatigues, and carries a 9mm Glock 17 pistol.

ДОЛГ·ЧЕСТЬ·ОТВАГА
СПЕЦНАЗ ВМФ

A selection of weapons used by the *Spetsnaz*. (From left to right): an SVDS sniper rifle, which is an advanced, folding-stock version of the regular SVD; a VSS Vintorez silenced sniper rifle; an AK-74 assault rifle; an AKM with GP-25 grenade-launcher; a 7.62mm AKMN with PBS sound suppressor; and a PKP Pecheneg general-purpose machine gun. (© Vitaly Kuzmin)

Spetsnaz, as well as other potential replacements such as the 9mm OTs-14-4 bullpup, each time the cost of rearming the military (at a time when Russia has massive stocks of unused AK-74s) has meant that these plans have been shelved for the foreseeable future.

Snipers play a key role in Spetsnaz tactics. While some still use the Soviet-era 7.62mm SVD Dragunov, and the modernized SVDS folding-stock version originally designed for the paratroopers, Spetsnaz increasingly use the 7.62mm SV-98, a bolt-action weapon typically mounting a PKS-07 7x fixed-magnification telescopic sight or a 1P69 3–10x42 variable-magnification optic, which give a range of out to 1000m (1,110 yds) in trained hands. Although the SV-98 can be fitted with a sound suppressor, the Spetsnaz are much more likely to use the VSS Vintorez rifle for missions where the need for stealth outweighs that for long-range accuracy. This specialized silenced rifle firing a heavy 9x39mm round has become something of a Spetsnaz trademark, especially as it was widely deployed in Crimea. It is part of a whole suite of silenced weapons favored by the Spetsnaz; others are the 9mm AS Val assault carbine, and the PB 6P9 pistol – a dated weapon based on the 1950s-vintage Makarov, but still issued for special missions. The SR-3 Vikhr is a shortened variant of the AS Val, which can be fitted with a suppressor but still fires the same subsonic round. Spetsnaz also used suppressed versions of the APS Stechkin pistol and the AK-74 and AK-47 rifles.

Support weapons

While Spetsnaz will more often operate as mechanized infantry than their Western counterparts, nonetheless they tend not to deploy with anything heavier than squad weapons, relying on attached units for artillery and other

support. The 7.62mm PKP 6P41 Pecheneg machine gun is their primary squad weapon; depending upon the mission, they are also issued with RPG-27 Tavolga and RPG-29 Vampir shoulder-fired antitank rocket-launchers, RPG-26 Arlen and RPG-30 Kryuk disposable rockets, RPO-A Shmel incendiary rocket-launchers, and SA-24 9K338 Igla-S man-portable surface-to-air missiles. They often mount GP-25 6G15 or GP-30 6G21 single-shot grenade-launchers on their rifles, and in some cases use the 6G30 "revolver" grenade-launcher firing the same 40mm VOG-25 rounds.

The 7.62mm PKP 6P41 Pecheneg general-purpose machine gun, a modernized version of the venerable PK, is widely used by the Russian armed services. It is the heaviest machine gun that *Spetsnaz* are likely to carry in the field, and so is a crucial source of firepower. (© Vitaly Kuzmin)

Personal kit

As befits their status, the Spetsnaz were among the first Russian troops to be issued the new Ratnik ("Warrior") personal equipment suite, including not just digital Flora-pattern camouflaged battledress designed to be more comfortable and durable than the previous issue, but also the 6B47 Kevlar combat helmet, 6B43 body armor, and a range of additional elements from elbow- and kneepads to hydration pouches. Some of the more advanced elements of the Ratnik suite, such as new-generation night-vision equipment, are still not yet ready for general issue. In Crimea in early 2014 Spetsnaz were seen using new 168-0,5UME personal radios – a leap forward for an army that has neglected modern tactical communications.

Despite their short effective ranges of 300–400m (330–440 yds), the *Spetsnaz* favor such sound-suppressed weapons as the 9mm AS Val assault carbine (top), firing subsonic armor-piercing rounds, and the VSS Vintorez sniper rifle. Both are products of the TsNIITochMash design bureau and the TOZ Tula Arms Works. (© Vitaly Kuzmin)

Close combat

The standard Russian combat sidearm is the 9mm GSh-18 pistol, and the Spetsnaz will use this for personal defense, as well as (rarely) 9mm submachine guns such as the Bizon, 9A-91, and Vityaz-SN. For even closer combat the Spetsnaz are issued either the 6Kh5 AK-74 bayonet-knife, or the NRS-2. The

Unarmed combat is a key element of *Spetsnaz* training, as much for physical and mental conditioning as for its utility in combat. Here scouts from the *razvedchik* company of the 27th Independent Motor Rifle Brigade demonstrate a Sambo throw. (© Vitaly Kuzmin)

Spetsnaz lore holds that the worst enemy a clandestine scout can face is a dog – trained, implacable, fast, and ferocious. Accordingly, they too use combat dogs for a wide range of tasks, from base security to sniffing out enemy booby traps. Most, like this German Shepherd, are bred and trained by the Army's 70th Cynological Center. (© Vitaly Kuzmin)

latter is the so-called "shooting scout knife," which incorporates in the hilt a single-shot mechanism firing a low-power 7.62mm bullet to an effective range of around 25m (80ft). (It is a Western myth that Spetsnaz used a ballistic knife with a powerful spring able to project its blade at an enemy.) The NRS-2 was issued from the 1980s, but it remains more a curio than a combat weapon, and is very rarely used as anything other than a regular knife. Indeed, many Spetsnaz prefer the NR-2 version, in which the firing mechanism is replaced by a compartment for survival tools.

On the other hand, the Spetsnaz do make use of their fabled *saperka*, technically the MPL or "small infantry shovel." A short-handled entrenching tool that is typically kept sharpened, this can either be used as a hand-to-hand weapon or thrown. While this tool is standard issue to all Russian troops, the Spetsnaz (and to an extent the VDV) do make a distinct sport of it, and not only train in its combat use but put on showy displays involving such feats as hurling the MPL at a target while leaping through a blazing hoop.

Closer in yet, the Spetsnaz are also extensively trained in unarmed combat, specifically the system called Sambo, a contraction of *Samozashchita bez oruzhiya*, "self-defense without weapons." This is a martial art that began to be developed by the Red Army as early as the 1920s, drawing on both traditional Russian wrestling and judo and jujitsu. It was from the first explicitly a combat art, and while it has since also evolved into a competitive sport, in its purest form it is strikingly devoid of any constraints

or philosophy beyond taking down the enemy as quickly and efficiently as possible. It thus encourages any kind of attack or – despite its name – the use of whatever formal or improvised weapon may come to hand. (The present author has watched Spetsnaz in training bouts use everything from bottles to street signs.)

Underwater equipment

Given the environment in which they operate, it is perhaps unsurprising that it is the Naval Spetsnaz who have the most distinctive equipment. They operate both above and below the surface; for the latter they use not just Protei-5 one-man diver propulsion vehicles, but also minisubmarines such as the Piranya (which can carry six operators for some 1500km/930 miles), and the smaller two-man Triton-1.

The underwater value of conventional firearms is extremely limited, and conventional spearguns also suffer from short range and indifferent accuracy, so the Naval Spetsnaz have acquired specialized weapons. Their combat swimmers use two such guns, designed in Soviet times: the SPP-1M pistol, and the APS rifle. The former is a four-barreled weapon that fires 4.5mm steel darts for 5m–20m (16–65ft) underwater, depending on the depth. The latter fires larger 5.66mm metal flechettes some 30m (100ft) in shallow water (down to no deeper than 11m/35ft) or 100m (330ft) when out of the water. Given the marginal performance of these weapons above the surface, Spetsnaz on raiding missions also often have to carry their regular weapons in waterproof cases. For this reason they adopted the ASM-DT Morskoi Lev ("Sea Lion") combination weapon in 2000. This rifle can switch between conventional 5.45mm ammunition and similar-caliber darts, allowing performance broadly comparable to the APS underwater and the AKS-74U carbine on dry land. However, whether because of financial constraints or problems in its design, to date this hybrid weapon appears to have been issued only very rarely.

SELECT BIBLIOGRAPHY

Burgess, William (ed.), *Inside Spetsnaz* (Presidio, 1990)

Galeotti, Mark, *Russian Security and Paramilitary Forces since 1991*, Elite 197 (Osprey, 2013)

Kolpakidi, Aleksandr and Aleksandr Sever, *Spetsnaz GRU. Samaya polnaya entsiklopediya* (Yauza, 2012)

Kozlov, Sergei, *Spetsnaz GRU. Ocherkii istorii. Vols 1–5* (Russkaya panorama, 2010–13)

Leonov, Viktor, *Blood on the Shores* (Ivy, 1994)

Schofield, Carey, *The Russian Elite* (Greenhill, 1993)

Skrynnikov, Mikhail, *Spetsnaz VDV* (Yauza, 2005)

Starinov, Ilya, *Over the Abyss: my life in Soviet special operations* (Ivy, 1995)

Strekhnin, Yuriy, *Commandos from the Sea: Soviet naval Spetsnaz in World War II* (Naval Institute Press, 1996)

Suvorov, Viktor, *Aquarium* (Hamish Hamilton, 1985)

Suvorov, Viktor, *Spetsnaz* (Norton, 1988)

INDEX

Page numbers in **bold** refer to illustrations and their captions.